BOB MOFFATT'S
POWER
LINES

BOB MOFFETT'S
POWER LINES

SCRIPTURE UNION
130 City Road, London EC1V 2NJ

© 1989 Scripture Union
130 City Road, London EC1V 2NJ

First published 1989

ISBN 0 86201 527 8

Except where otherwise shown, Scripture quotations in this
publication are from the Holy Bible, New International
Version. Copyright © 1973, 1978, 1984 International Bible
Society. Published by Hodder and Stoughton.

British Library Cataloguing in Publication Data
Moffett, Bob
   Power lines
   1. Young persons.   Christian life
   I. Title
   248.8'3

   ISBN 0-86201-527-8

Artwork by Simon Jenkins.
Cover design and illustration by Tony Cantale Graphics and
Simon Jenkins.

Typeset by Input Typesetting Ltd, London
Printed in Great Britain
at the University Press, Oxford

CONTENTS

BECOMING MORE LIKE CHRIST

SPECIAL OCCASIONS

Dedicated to George Brucks who has led me
into unusual and creative paths across the
landscapes of Europe!

Preface

'Power Lines' was not written for you but for me! Like
you, as a youth leader I am in the business of
survival. . . trying to produce regular, creative
programmes for young people. I want them to learn more
about the God of the Bible, the God of creation and to
learn to love the Lord Jesus Christ.

Please adapt the material in this book for your group
but please do not skimp in your preparation by adapting
it so much that your part in the preparation becomes
minimal!

My thanks **again** go to Jilly, my wife, for the hours of
her time that I have wasted in bouncing some rather
stupid ideas off her in preparing these outlines!

Twelve of the outlines were originally published in
'Buzz' magazine (now '21st Century Christian') as
'Power Pages'. My thanks go to Hilary Saunders for
permission to reprint them, and to Gill Smith for her
editorial work on them. Becky Totterdell has edited this
book in a most helpful fashion, giving lively suggestions
to communicate my often haphazard ideas.

I love young people. God loves them much more. For
God's sake, please do not sell them short – be both
creative and wise as you lead your young people closer
to the God of the Bible.

Bob Moffett

Introduction

How often do you go out for a slap-up five-course meal?
Once a week? Once a month? Very occasionally? Just
imagine how ridiculous it would be if you depended
entirely on those meals to keep you going, and spent
the long periods in between fasting!

Yet for so many Christians in Britain, that is the extent
of their spiritual diet! They fill themselves to bulging
point at church conferences, house-parties and special
teaching weeks – then rely on snacks and nibbles until
the next biblical banquet comes along.

This book is like a filing cabinet of menu cards for
Christians in that kind of situation. Maybe your young
people get back to church after a mouth-watering feast,
with a big appetite to learn more about God's plan for
their lives, only to go hungry because there is no planned
diet to satisfy them. The outlines here aim to provide
small groups of young people, interested in studying the
Bible together, with a fresh, down-to-earth approach.
The studies will not give all the answers, but will attempt
to stimulate the group's thinking on subjects which
directly affect their daily lives.

Four of the outlines in this book are for YOU – the
youth group leader – to help you assess the success of
your own leadership style. Of the thirty-two others, you
will find that many can be split into two for use over
two weeks. Feel free to add your own ideas into the
programmes, too.

FOR THE LEADER

What on earth am I doing?

Bill has been 'doing' his club now for two years and, in his words, it's going 'OK.' The minister seems to be happy because Bill doesn't complain and the few youngsters he has seem quite satisfied – though he doesn't think that the youngsters he started out with are the same ones that he's got now. 'But maybe I'm wrong,' he says, making a note to check some time.

GROUP SURVEY

Now this may not be your situation, but *who* checks on your progress using clear criteria? Part of our problem is that few people are trained to help in the area of youth development. So *you* need to do this exercise yourself. Taken together, the survey in this outline and the guidelines for action in the next will help you:
1 to identify what kind of group you are;
2 to discuss this important ministry with your church leadership;
3 to set some realistic goals.

Begin by completing the following survey.

Your group

1 What type of youth group do you lead or help lead?
- [ ] Youth fellowship
- [ ] Uniformed organization
- [ ] Bible study
- [ ] Social group
- [ ] Other

2 What age range does the group comprise?
- [ ] 12–15
- [ ] 15–20
- [ ] 20–25

3 What is the male/female ratio?

4 How many attend the youth meeting on average?

5 Where do you meet?

6 What area is your church situated in?
- [ ] Inner city
- [ ] Urban
- [ ] Suburban
- [ ] Rural

7 Approximately how many of your group are the following?

Students ....
School pupils ....
Unemployed ....
Employed ....

8 What percentage of your group are the following?

Committed Christians ....
Searching ....
Just come along for the friendship ....

You and your style

1 What is your age?

2 How many people are involved in running the youth group?

3 How would you describe your leadership style?
- [ ] Dictatorial
- [ ] Work through delegation
- [ ] Democratic
- [ ] Laissez-faire

4 Does your group 'breed' its own leaders, or does everybody depend on you?

1

5 How long do you spend preparing each session?

☐ 0–1 hour each week

☐ 1–2 hours

☐ 2–3 hours

☐ over 3 hours

6 What resource material do you use?

....

....

7 Have you received any form of regular training for your youth ministry?

....

8 How often do you meet with your other leaders in the church to discuss related youth issues?

....

9 Do you receive a youth budget from the church? If so does it meet your requirements?

....

10 What do you find most problematic about your youth work?
(Use another sheet of paper if necessary!)

....

....

11 What do you find most rewarding?

....

....

12 How often do you meet with your minister to discuss your youth work?

....

13 How often do you meet with the leaders of other youth organizations to discuss youth work issues?

Your programme

1 What is the aim of your group?

....

2 How often do you make a programme for meetings?

....

3 Do you set goals for your group?

If so, are they measurable?

....

4 If you set goals, what period of time do you set them for?

☐ A term

☐ A year

☐ Other

5 Do you ever achieve any of these goals?

....

6 Are you going through a Bible series? If so what?

....

7 What is the biggest social issue facing your group at the moment?

☐ Unemployment

☐ Sex and relationships

☐ Exams

☐ Home life

☐ Other

....

8 Have you had a specialist in to talk about any of these issues?

....

9 What spiritual issues are your group facing right now?

☐ Accepting Christ

☐ Discovering the Holy Spirit

☐ Building up a prayer life

☐ Other

....

10 How have you dealt with them?

....

11 Did your last programme of activities contain an evangelistic event?

....

Relationships

1 Is your group involved in any social activities outside of the church? If so, what?

....

2 Is your group involved in the life of the church?

....

3 How would you describe your church's attitude towards the youth group?

....

4 Are you involved with other churches in the area on a special or spiritual basis? If so, which and on what basis?

....
....
....

2 How on earth am I going to pull this together?

Bill reluctantly completes the survey in the first outline and feels depressed. It looks pretty bad. But in fact he has just done the best thing he could have for himself, his youth group, and for God's work in it. But what should Bill do with it now?

GUIDELINES FOR ACTION

If Bill takes the results of his survey to his church leadership they may think he is trying to make trouble, as it may look too negative. But if he *really* wants to worry them, he should go in with some positive ideas for change and progress! He will have to be careful though . . . they might ask him to organize the rest of the church as well!

This, however, is a bit of a jaundiced view of church leadership! Most ministers or leadership teams will want to help Bill in whatever way he would like them to help. So what *would* he

really like to see his youth group become, in order to be the best that it could be for God and the young people?

Take a leaf out of Bill's book and work through the guidelines below:

Steps to achieving your dreams

1 Spend time with God

● Plan to spend a morning or day away from everything to think and pray about the youth group.

● Tell the Lord all about the youth group: your frustrations and successes; where you feel he has

not supported you; the times you wanted to give it up . . . the times you did!

● Ask the Lord to help you 'dream' about what it *could* be like: what if you took seriously the support of praying people? What type of youth meeting would you really love to see? What role in it do you really wish you were taking? How would the young people be developing?

2 Plan carefully

● Write down what you have just 'dreamt' about the way the youth work could be.

● Pray for wisdom as you now proceed down a very significant road.

● Plan your **long-term aims and goals**. Think into the future – twelve months ahead – and list the things you would like to see in your youth group/programme/yourself by then. These are your long-term

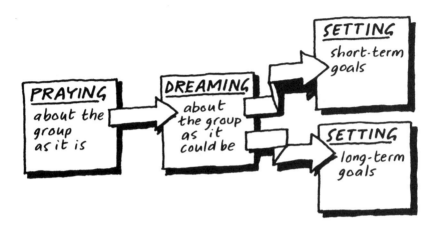

aims. Then ask yourself, 'What do I need to plan to make those dreams come true?' List the things you will have to plan. These are your long-term **goals**. They should be measurable: you know whether you have done them or not. For instance, your **aim** may be to see numerical growth, so your **goal** may be to choose and train other leaders. Your **aim** may be to see your group enthused and excited about being a Christian, so your **goal** may be to take them to one of the big Christian festivals. Your **aim** may be to see your group contributing more to church life, so

your **goal** could be to plan a Christmas drama with your youth group, to be performed for the church as a whole. Your **aim** may be to see your young people grow spiritually, and be able to think through difficult issues for themselves. So your **goal** may be to tackle some difficult issues with the group.

Write down your **aims** and your **long-term goals** in two columns (see chart).

● Set yourself **short-term goals**. These are the things you need to do *now* in order to hit your long-term goals. For example, if you are going

to choose and train more leaders, you will need to start thinking now about who might be suitable. The best thing to do may be to talk this over with your minister or vicar, who may have spotted potential in someone you would overlook. You will also need to ask God to guide you to the right person/people. So your short-term goal might look like this:

'Make an appointment with vicar to talk over possible leaders. Pray for clear guidance.'

Carry on setting yourself short-term goals, listing them in a third column beside your long-term goals.

3 Be bold

Act as if **God** is in charge – which of course he is – and as if you have committed your ways and plans to him – which of course you have. As God directs your plans you can be certain that he is working his purposes out even if he doesn't choose to follow your ideas to the letter.

4 Pray

Get your friends praying; get the young people praying – but be creative. Plan your praying just like everything else. If you do not, the devil will make sure that you plan it out of your schedule altogether!

I would strongly recommend that you buy *Prayer Pace-setting*, by John Earwicker, published by Scripture Union. It is designed to help you and your group be creative as you pray.

IMPORTANT: Do not forget to relate all the above to the survey in outline 1.

AIMS	LONG-TERM GOALS	SHORT-TERM GOALS
1 Numerical growth.	1 Choose and train new leaders.	1 Make an appointment with vicar to talk over possible leaders. Pray for guidance.
2 Enthuse the group about being Christians.	2 Take them to an enthusiasm-engendering Christian festival.	2 Find out what is on and when. Book now.
3 To have group contributing more to church life.	3 Plan a Christmas drama for the Sunday family service.	3 Discuss possibilities with vicar. Look out good material.
4 To have the young people growing spiritually and emotionally.	4 Tackle some of the important issues, maybe with help of outside speaker.	4 Plan which issues; invite and book outside speakers.
5 To be a better youth leader!	5 Do some training.	5 Write off to training organizations.

Getting into gear

Successful people are those who plan their work. So why is it that some of those who do this successfully for their work outside church do not appear to bring their planning abilities into the church?!

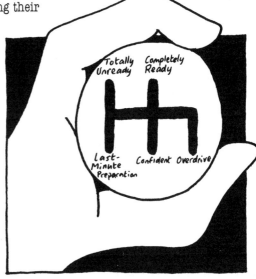

To add that extra dimension of success to your youth programme, make a plan for each meeting, well in advance of it happening. This way you will feel on top of things at the time, and be relaxed enough to hear God's voice speaking to you as you go along.

Here is an outline plan for you to complete.

THE 'IT' MEETING

Date: .... Time: .... Venue: ....

Title of meeting: ....

Subject of meeting: ....

3

Purpose of meeting:
(What do I want the group to do, or how do I want them to be changed, as a result of the meeting?)

....

....

PREPARATION

Publicity required:

....

....

....

People not there last week whom I need to remind:

....

....

....

Preparation I need to make:

....

....

....

Preparation others/the group need to make:

....

....

....

Crowdbreakers:

....

....

....

PROGRAMME

Introduction
How will I introduce the subject? (Key phrases, activities, etc.)

....

....

....

3

Content
How will I present the main points? (Key phrases, Bible sources, quotes, crowdbreakers, experience activities, discussion, video, question and answer, etc.) List main points and method of presentation in order.

....

....

....

....

....

....

....

Summary
How will I conclude the session? (Key phrases, activities, etc.)

....

....

....

Checklist
(Things I will need to bring.)
- Bibles
- Paper
- Pens
- Flip chart
- Overhead projector
- Refreshments
- Crowdbreaker-props
- Video
- Slide projector and screen
- Mains leads

NB: Pray!!

After the meeting

My reaction and assessment:

....

....

The group's reaction and assessment:

....

....

4

Help!

Most youth leaders are overworked and totally unpaid! In this session and the next we will be considering how to get help and use volunteers in the youth group.

If you need help, do not ask for volunteers; choose them (Jesus did.) If you ask for a volunteer, the very fact that you are having to ask for help comes across negatively. You need to *choose* a leadership team.

ASK DAD

One of the best resources for encouragement, information and background assistance are the parents of the young people. Do some market research. Get some feedback. Use a questionnaire like the one below to gain an invaluable insight into the minds of the young people; learn about them from the views of their parents!

How to go about it

● Design your questionnaire. (Use the one shown here to start you thinking.)

● Give time to its preparation and have it typed.

● Do not be afraid to send it to non-Christian parents or parents of non-Christian members of the group.

● Tell your youth group/fellowship members that you are sending it.

● Post it to the parents with a stamped addressed envelope and a short hand-written note of explanation – keep it light!

PARENT QUESTIONNAIRE

Name ....

Tel ....

Young person involved: Name .... Age ....

School ....

HELP US TO HELP YOUR CHILD

What is of most importance to you at present, or causing the most problems, in relation to your son/daughter? Number the items listed below in order of importance, '1' being the most important.

- [ ] Parent/teenager conflict
- [ ] Understanding the teenagers' world
- [ ] Teaching them Christian standards
- [ ] Being a parent
- [ ] Family devotions
- [ ] Understanding Christianity
- [ ] The teenager at school
- [ ] How to help my child get a job
- [ ] Money in the home
- [ ] Relationships between brother/sister
- [ ] Other

HELP US TO EVALUATE

1 What do you like most about the youth meeting your child(ren) attends?

2 What do you dislike most about it?
3 How do you feel about the leadership?
4 What would you like to see changed in the next six months?
5 What aspect of the youth meeting does your child(ren) talk about more than anything else (besides it being boring)?

HELP US TO DO IT BETTER

1 Are you occasionally able to provide transport? If so, for how many and how often?
2 Would you be willing for us to use your home three times this year? How many could you fit in comfortably/uncomfortably?

HELP US TO UNDERSTAND

Please complete these sentences:

1 Young people today are . . .
2 The most important thing for the family is . . .
3 If I were to describe my relationship with my children in a few words it would be . . .
4 God is . . .
5 The church is . . .
Please help us by adding any other comments. Thank you!

Please note:
The completed questionnaire will not be shown to your child(ren) unless **you** show it to them.

FUTURE SHOCK

Summer, particularly August, can be a crucial decision time for young people.

It's the month when they find out whether they have passed GCSE and 'A' level exams and what grades they got – all of which will shape their future. Disastrous results may mean a huge rethink for those who thought they would be going off to college or university.

For others it is a big decision time on whether to study for exams at all – do they want to knuckle down and work next term? Would they be better looking for a job now or staying on to get further qualifications?

PROGRAMME

Road signs

Ask your group to choose two signs: one which best reflects where they see themselves now and one which states where they want to get to in the coming year.

Give them time to reflect and make their choice. It would be helpful to give each person a piece of paper to write down why they chose their signs. You should also join in this exercise.

In small groups ask people to explain to each other why they chose these particular road signs. But there should be no pressure on anyone to express their views if they do not want to.

PREPARATION

Get hold of some highway symbols. Either draw them out on paper with a thick felt pen or ask your local authority if they have any old posters or pictures of highway code signs.

Alternatively your group's 'photographer' might like to go out and photograph some. Obviously this will have to be done in advance to allow time for developing.

Place your road signs round the room.

This session's material is designed to help your young people come to terms with the way they are feeling about life at this time.

Make sure that you read out your list of reasons for choosing the signs you did. To show that there is no pressure on anyone, tell them if there are one or two things on the list which you wrote down but which you are keeping confidential.

For example, in Mark 1:4–13 Jesus is at something like a red light – he could not start his ministry yet. It was not until his baptism that he was given the 'green light' to go ahead.

Bible signposts

Tell the group that there were significant points in the life and ministry of Jesus that were like road signs on the way. Sometimes he was confronted with something like a crossroad which made him make a deliberate choice. At other times the signs were a real encouragement on the way.

Still in small groups, give out copies of the following verses and ask them to answer two questions:
● What is the significant road sign (not literally) in each verse?
● What did it mean for Jesus? How did it change his thinking or action?

The verses are all in Mark's Gospel: 1:4–13; 14–20; 21–28; 2:1–12; 6:1–5 and 6:7–13.

Commandments

The Ten Commandments can all be portrayed as road signs so, as a final exercise, get the small groups to make a road sign for each of the Ten Commandments. If you only have one or two groups, then you may need to select just a couple of commandments.

For example, 'You shall not give false testimony against your neighbour' could be shown as the warning of a slippery road:

These should be drawn on large sheets of paper and, if good, could be plastered around the church walls next Sunday. Maybe if there is someone artistically inclined in the group he or she could tidy them up a bit before public viewing.

Twenty years on  6

Two years ago I would not even have thought about moving to the Middle East with my family.

Twelve years ago I would never have thought I would be as involved in youth ministry as I am now.

Twenty years ago I was a mere teenager and had very little idea of what I wanted to do except 'serve God somehow'.

In fact, I thought that to be a real Christian and to grow spiritually I should apply to become a priest! Four years later I did apply – and was turned down!

Where do the young people in your youth group want to be in five, ten or twenty years' time? It is an unfair question in many ways as our plans do not always come to fruition; and yet we must encourage young people to dream, and must prepare them for 'vocations'.

PROGRAMME

Future thoughts

Ask your group to think into the future, not about society as a whole but about themselves.

If they are seventeen years or over, ask them to think fifteen years ahead. If they are sixteen or under ask them to think twenty years ahead. You will need to prompt them with questions like:

• Will you be married/divorced/single?
• Will you have children? How many?
• Where will you be living, and what in?
• Will you still be involved with the church?
• Will God have a place in your thinking?
• Will you have a job?
• Will you still be in touch with your family?

The above are just some of the examples you may wish to use. It would be helpful to have them written up as guidelines.

Give each person a piece of paper and ask them to write down their ideas. They have eleven minutes in which to do this.

They should then place their paper in an envelope which you have provided, seal it and put their name on it. The envelope should be marked: 'What I think I will be doing in fifteen or twenty years' time', and passed to you.

6

Angela
What I'll be doing
in 20 years.

Questions
1 What important things should we do now which will determine who we are in the future?
2 How does God view our future?
3 What do we do now to ensure a fulfilled life in the future?

Role play
Ask each member of your group in turn to go out of the room and prepare a short role-play based on what they wrote in their letter. Each person comes back into the room and the group welcomes him or her as if they have not seen them for fifteen years. They ask questions of the individual, such as 'What are you doing now? Are you married?'

However, the group should respond to the individual's answers in the light of the relationship they had with them fifteen years ago. For example, if the individual says, 'I am a world-famous brain surgeon', and the others know he or she got an ungraded GCSE in biology they should point this out.

The aim of this exercise is to find out what *your group* think their friends will be doing in the future rather than what the individual thinks. There is often a difference between the way we see ourselves and the way others see us.

Alternative: you may prefer to have the individual come back into the group and let the others just tell him or her what they think he or she has been doing for the last fifteen years.

The Bible and the future
Divide the group into three, and give each group one of the following passages of the Bible to look at. Ask them to answer the questions which follow (give them eight minutes to do this). Have a short feedback session so that they can share their findings with the others.
● Ephesians 4:17–32 (Putting off and putting on)
● Luke 12:13–21 (Building barns)
● 1 Corinthians 6:18–20 (You are not your own)

Another letter
Give out another piece of paper and ask them to do exactly the same thing as they did at the beginning but this time they should address this letter, 'Dear God. . .'

In light of what their friends have said and also what they have read from the Bible, they should tell God how they would like to be in fifteen or twenty years' time.

This letter should again be put into an envelope, and marked: 'Dear God, from . . . (in fifteen or twenty years' time).'

Give them back their original envelope and give them the option as to which envelope they wish to tear up. The other envelope should be returned to you with the promise that you will give it back to them in one or two years' time, wherever they are!

Keep to your word and this session may still have effect long after the meeting.

What's on your mind?

Getting young people to express themselves is no mean feat. Some sit there looking so vacant that you want to hang a sign around their necks saying 'gone away'.

Others are so articulate that politicians' speeches sound like nursery rhymes in comparison!

There are others who will pour out their souls at the slightest opportunity and still others who squirm over every word, like a rattlesnake going backwards up a mountainside.

This session brings you a game which helps your group to open up about their feelings. It will also give you an opportunity to discover your youth group's views on a wide range of subjects.

> 15 serious questions
> 15 light-hearted questions
> 4 cards saying 'Comment'
> 4 cards saying 'Question'
> 2 blank cards

PREPARATION

Buy a number of small index cards, preferably of two different colours. Split the cards into their respective colours and on one set write out some serious questions and on the other more light-hearted questions. (See 'On My Mind' boxes for examples.)

The following numbers of cards will make up one complete pack of cards. (You may need more than one pack depending on the size of your group: one pack to eight players, and one leader to each group of eight players.)

Put the serious and light-hearted cards in separate piles and add two 'Question', two 'Comment' and one blank card to each pile.

PROGRAMME

To play
1 Divide the group into eights – more or less.
2 Sit each group in a position where they are reasonably close to each other.
3 Each person in turn should throw a die. If an even number is thrown, the player picks up a 'serious' card; an odd number gets him or her a 'light-hearted' card.
4 As a person draws a card he or she speaks for no more than two or three sentences on the topic given, giving their own views.
5 If a player picks up a 'Question' or a 'Comment' card, that player can ask someone else in the group a question or ask them to make a comment on any subject of their choice.
6 Receiving a blank card means you can either pass or say anything you like on any subject.
7 The activity should last no more than about forty minutes and the pace of the comments should be relatively quick but not to the exclusion of serious thought.
8 Naturally, cards are placed face downwards so that the participants cannot see the topic before they pick up the card.
9 Each person should read out their topic card before proceeding.

7

Summarize

Bring the groups together again after the forty to forty-five minutes are up. Explain to them that Jesus is interested in their views and their private thoughts.

Some people came to Jesus quietly so that others would not know. Nicodemus was one (John 3). Other people came to Jesus with very definite opinions (Luke 11:37–44). Others came to Jesus because they wanted to discuss their views (The Rich Young Ruler, Luke 18:18–30). Others rejected Jesus' advice and actions (John 11:45–57).

Our ideas, God's ideas

The best thing to do with all our views is to *discuss them with Jesus* in prayer. Even if you are finding the Christian faith difficult you can still talk to Jesus about it.

The Bible can help us work through our ideas about issues. Reading about how God spoke to his people in the past helps us get a better idea of the way God's views relate to our situation.

Other people can help us work out difficult issues in our lives. People we trust and who know us well – youth leader, house group leaders, etc – can often shed light on things.

ON MY MIND (SERIOUS TOPICS)

- Is there anything which is upsetting you?
- What embarrasses you?
- Which two people are closest to you? Why?
- How is your relationship with God?
- What do you find most difficult about the Christian life?
- 'When I am criticized I . . .'
- Do your parents understand you? Explain.
- What three major problems do young people face today?
- Share your ideas about abortion.
- What do you feel about the poor in the world?

ON MY MIND (LIGHT-HEARTED TOPICS)

- My favourite meal is . . .
- I would spend an unexpected fortune on . . .
- Talk about one of your bad habits.
- What is your favourite pop group and why?
- If you could change your name what would it be?
- Who would you take to a desert island?
- Who was your favourite teacher and why?
- What is your favourite TV show? Why?
- When I dream I think of . . .
- My favourite hymn is . . .

Reaction cards

Finally, give each group member a card on which they can write down their honest reaction to the meeting, stating if it has helped them or made them think.

The cards should be passed back to you anonymously but make it clear if someone would like to discuss an issue with you they should put their name on the card.

Stress

Stress, pressure, anxiety. As a youth group leader, you probably experience all these emotions as you prepare for, pray over and worry about youth group nights.
But have you ever thought about the stress which the young people in your group also experience?

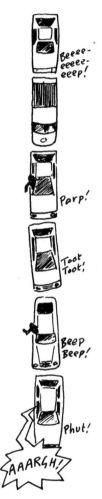

It is not a phenomenon restricted to the nine-till-five working, mortgage-paying, car-owning, polyunsaturate-conscious commuter. It is there among the under twenty-one's – pressure to do well in exams, worry about being different from their peer group, difficulties at home and in relationships.

Before you go through this session on stress with your youth group, you will have to discuss with them what you mean by stress factors, that is, the events in our daily lives which cause us to show stress symptoms: headaches, short temper, depression, even physical illness.

PROGRAMME

Producing stress

Begin by playing some games designed to induce a mild level of stress in the group:

● **Loaded mousetrap.** Divide the group into teams. The members of each team line up, one behind the other. The first person in each must carry a loaded, well-oiled mousetrap to a certain line and back and then pass it on to the next person, who carries it to the line and back again. This process is repeated down the team. If the trap springs (this will occur often), that player must start again. The team which finishes first is given a knob of cheese as a reward.

● **Russian egg roulette.** Select five pairs. One partner takes an egg and breaks it over the other's head simultaneously with the other pairs. Four of the eggs are hard-boiled and one is raw. One person is in for a messy time. If you consider this too messy, poke a hole in the raw egg and drain out its contents. Refill the egg with water and set it with clear wax.

● **Voluntary fear.** This is probably at its best when played after a nasty game. This is not a game at all, just a way of creating tension. Ask for two volunteers and send them out of the room. Tell the rest that when you call in the volunteers nothing at all is going to happen; you are just going to ask them to sit down in their places and carry on as if nothing has happened. Instruct your group to say nothing if they are asked anything by the volunteers.

The unknown, the fear of what might happen, makes the volunteers very uneasy and therefore makes an excellent discussion starter for later on when you come to talk about fears.

8

● **Breaking point.** Divide the entire group into pairs and give each pair a large rubber band (all rubber bands should be identical). If you have room, line the pairs up in two lines facing each other; if you are crowded, let them stand anywhere.

Each person in the pair places a finger inside the rubber band. At your command, each person takes a step backward (steps should be the length of the person's foot). Continue one step at a time until the bands break. The last remaining rubber band stretched – but not broken – wins.

Paper stress

Ask each person to list all their anxieties on a piece of paper (anonymous). Examples which may arise are: Failure – examinations; Parents – splitting up, arguing, fighting; Future – job, relationships, death, loneliness, rape, guilt, money. List them on a board after collecting the sheets. This is important because it helps people to realise that others have similar worries.

On another piece of paper they should list their worries in priority order – the most worrying as number one. This is important because it allows them to see what is really worrying them.

Bible stress

Split your group into units and give each the following Bible passages to discuss. Ask them to answer the question: What practical advice do these verses give. . .

● 1 John 4:7–12
. . . about relating to others?
● John 16:32–33
. . . when everyone appears to be against us?
● Ephesians 4:26–32
. . . about handling anger?
● Matthew 6:25–34
. . . on money problems?
● James 1:2–4
. . . about facing problems?
● Philippians 4:4–7
. . . on everything?

Stressing the point

Using their individual priority stress/anxiety sheet, get your group to write against their first five stress factors what practical steps they are going to take to alleviate that stress. Give them examples such as the two below.

Church stress

Arrange for your group to go round the church members, asking them, sensitively, what things make them worry. Record their answers. Edit the tape for short, pithy comments and use it to give a fifteen minute presentation on stress in one of your normal Sunday services.

STRESS	PRIORITY NUMBER	PRACTICAL STEPS
Failure	6	
Future	4	
Death	1	I'm going to thank God that I already have eternal life, and that death is just a transition.
Guilt	5	
Money	7	
Loneliness	2	I noticed from looking over Pete's paper (I know that I shouldn't have done it) that he gets lonely too. I could talk to him about it.

The wedding

Most of us will go to a wedding at some time or other – even if only our own!

Sometimes we really enjoy them; we know a lot of the people and are very pleased and happy for the bride and groom. At other times we might go to a wedding out of duty; smile at the right time for the photos, kiss the bride, have a nosh and then go home (and nearly forget to give the couple their present!).

PREPARATION

Ask your church leaders for a copy of the wedding service which is 'done' in your church – and have a wedding.

Announce the week before that everybody has got to get dressed up, but do not explain why. Ask them to meet at the church.

PROGRAMME

As people arrive have music playing from the organ, sit them near the front and have a wedding with the full works, but without the pronouncement of 'marriage' at the end.

Volunteer people as you go along: a bride, bride's father, groom, best man, bridesmaids.

As the bride and groom take the vows stop the proceedings after each one and ask the group what that vow means. Would they really want to make that kind of commitment?

Do not make this laborious but try to draw out their real feelings. You may be surprised to find that their ideals are higher than you think.

Christian wedding services have much biblical content. Go through this with the group, too. If you are using the Book of Common Prayer examine the first prayer of the service, which specifies the reasons for marriage.

Do tell your minister what you are proposing to do for this session. He may well want to play the part of the vicar!

Do not forget the reception!

10

With the benefit of hindsight

Mums and dads can find that all communication between themselves and their adolescent children has dried up. Parents may think this is the 'generation gap' appearing, the fault of the children drifting away from them. Teenagers may claim that it is their parents who are out of touch with today's world and cannot really relate to them on issues which young people feel are important.

However, some teenagers are able to communicate very openly with their parents. So, over the next two sessions, let us work on improving communication across the generations. We will invite parents and teenagers to talk together about the latter's favourite preoccupation: romance and love. This will also give young people the benefit of the adults' hindsight and so encourage them to think more carefully about their own future plans in this area.

PREPARATION

The week before this event, tell your group that you are going to have a romantic evening and that they should come suitably dressed, that is, 'clean'! Arrange to have this session in someone's home.

Invite two couples who may or may not be known to the group but who are good at communicating with each other and with other people. They are there to share their experiences of their own 'romance', how they got to know

each other, the things they did together, the reaction of their family, and so on.

It is important to go over this beforehand with the couples so that you can check what they are going to say and so be able to relax when the time comes for them to say it!

However, allow and encourage them to put their mistakes, too, before the young people as teenagers learn much of importance from observing older people. Devise with them some questions which you can give the group to ask them, in case the young people are too embarrassed to ask their own questions.

PROGRAMME

Set the scene for romance . . . soft lights, delicate music, food (you do not have to go overboard).

Have some red roses to give the girls as they come in. Arrange for someone else to take the coats of all the group and to then show them to the refreshments.

GENERATION GAP

Poetry

Hand out some good quality paper to each person, along with a pen, and ask each of them to write a 'love poem'. Emphasize that it does not matter whether they actually have a girlfriend or boyfriend; this is a way of getting 'into the mood' for this evening's subject.

To encourage them, read from the Song of Songs – all or part of chapter 4:1–11, for example. No doubt the group will find the comparisons quite amusing, particularly the comparisons for teeth (v2), hair (v1) and temples (v3)!

Ask some of them to read out their poems to the others, including at least one of the married couples you have brought in for the evening. The more 'soppy' the better!

Discussion

After this, hand out some questions which the young people are to ask about the romantic life of the married couples, their courtship and their marriage. The young people can of course ask other questions if they wish, and you should encourage them to do so, but giving out questions saves embarrassment if they do not know what to say. Make it clear, though, that there is one condition attached to asking questions: that if the person they ask prefers *not* to answer the question they can say 'pass' and no one will ask them about that issue again.

You know your group better than anyone else so do not hesitate to make up the relevant questions, but do not hesitate to get down to basics either.

Option

You may wish to split the lads from the girls and have the couples split so that the men answer the lads' questions and the women answer the questions of the girls. This may give a little more freedom but the aim of encouraging discussion and understanding between the sexes will not be so fully realized.

Biblical principles

Move on to ask the couples to explain the biblical principles which they tried to follow in establishing their relationship. They may find it helpful if you suggest some Bible passages to them beforehand which they could bring into their explanation. For example:

- 1 Corinthians 6:18–20
- 2 Corinthians 6:14–16
- 1 Corinthians 13
- Ephesians 5:22–32 (without getting into 'headship' controversy!)

Conclude the evening by thanking God for 'romance', for creating male and female and creating the concept of love.

Option

The young people could include, in this time of prayer, prayers for their future marriage partners whether known or unknown. Make it clear, though, that God may ask some of the group to be single and that this brings a different set of rewards and demands.

SUGGESTED QUESTIONS

- How did you meet?
- What did you like *best* about him/her?
- What did your parents think about this relationship?
- Have your parents changed their minds about your partner?
- Did you each pay when you went out?
- Did you discuss having children before you decided to get married?
- What did you *not* like about each other?
- What happens when you argue?
- What annoys the other about what you do? How do you sort out your disagreements?
- How did you know that you were meant for each other?
- Before you got married did you ever talk about getting divorced if it did not work out?
- Where did God fit into your thinking?
- Did you pray about your marriage?
- Why did you not just live together? Why did you bother with a church service?

11 Playing mums and dads

As children we played 'mums and dads' with all the realism we could muster at that tender age, organizing the children (dolls) and arguing and fighting like real mums and dads. Now, sadly, children also act out divorce and separation.

Once we get married, though, we do not find the fairy-tale world which we once acted out. Instead there are the pressures of holding down a job; living with someone else who is unlike me; children who do not always respond in the way we would like . . . particularly in public, in front of those we really wanted to impress! And then they turn into something called 'adolescents' and no one understands their peculiar emotions and behaviour.

Let's get the young people to look at themselves through the eyes of their parents.

PREPARATION

Invite to your meeting three or four couples who have teenagers. It would be ideal but not always practical to get them from outside your community; that is, they should not be the parents of teenagers who come to your youth fellowship or church.

PROGRAMME

Discussion

1 Split the teenagers from the parents and ask each group to write down some questions they would like to ask the other. For example, teenagers may want to know why the parents always ask them to be in at 'set' times. The parents may want to ask the teenagers why they go out looking really smart but are happy to leave their bedroom looking like a rubbish tip.

Give the groups fourteen minutes to do this and then ask them to hand each other their questions.

Still in their groups they should pool their brains to try to answer the questions the other group has set them.

2 Give them seventeen minutes to work out their answers, then bring the two groups back together so that the questions can be read out and answered by the spokesperson. Allow comments between questions and answers, but move on fairly quickly to the next question.

Naturally, if you have a large youth group, bring in more couples.

3 Read Ephesians 6:1–4 and/or Colossians 3:20–21. Split the group again into teenagers and parents and ask each to think about what these verses mean for 'the others': the teenagers should consider what these verses say to parents about the way they treat teenage children, and the parents should consider the verses' message for teenagers.

4 After ten minutes bring the groups back together again to share their findings.

Mistakes!

You need to prepare your parents for the next activity. The idea is to 'put them on the spot' and ask each of them to express in a few words:

● one mistake they made as a teenager

● one good decision they made as a teenager

Finish by asking two of the parents and two of the teenagers to pray for those in the other category. You will need to have arranged this with them beforehand.

Important!
When the groups come together f the question-and-answer sessions make sure that they are as integrated as possible. Do not let the parents huddle together in one corner and the teenagers in another!

WORKING TOGETHER

My church does everything right!

12

A thing is either right or wrong; it cannot be anything in between. You would probably not like to describe yourself as a person who thinks in such a dogmatic way. But if you are under eighteen years of age it is highly likely you do see things as being so clear-cut.

Sometimes it is good to think in this way on major doctrines like the authority of the Bible and the deity of Christ. But when it comes to issues of secondary importance, like church denomination, it is good to be more open-minded.

Our denominational views as youth leaders can be picked up by our young people and make them narrow-minded. So this session seeks unashamedly to undermine your denominational preferences and practices and, with your co-operation, to broaden your group's spectrum in thinking of the wider church.

Explain to your minister and/or elders what you will be doing, before engaging in this session; and give them the reasons for your plans. Be aware that you might unearth some long-held insecurities!

The programme is going to involve a lot of organization, mostly by you. Here is a list of ideas; you choose what you think will benefit your group.

MEET THE VICAR

Have your group ever sat down on a normal youth evening and asked your minister all those questions about the church that have been brewing for some time?

To do this sensitively and positively, the questions should be planned in advance at one of your

normal (or abnormal) meetings – preferably after a good, lively Bible study on the church. Let the minister have a copy of them before the youth meeting.

Questions like:
● Why are we different from other churches?
● What do we believe that others may not?
● What is your biggest frustration running a church?
● What do you like best about being a minister?
● How can we help in the church?

MEET THE VICAR NEXT DOOR

This is very similar to the meeting with your own minister. Visit another church and ask their minister what the church believes and practises. Again, prepare questions in advance. It may be good if the other minister had a couple of his youth leaders with him.

12

MEET THE YOUTH GROUP

Get together with your opposite number in another church and arrange an evening's activities which would be both social and devotional in nature.

Prepare activities where the groups can interact with each other in order to learn about each other's faith, worship, evangelism, prayer and Bible study. Better still, arrange a couple of such evenings with two different churches.

GO TO ANOTHER SERVICE

With the agreement of your own church leadership, plan your absence and visit another church *en masse*. Give advance warning so that your group will be properly welcomed.

Plan to have a meeting with the minister of the church afterwards over a cup of coffee so that he can answer questions about the service.

ALL TOGETHER NOW

Attempt to have a lively fellowship meeting for all the youth fellowships of the local churches, after the Sunday evening service.

Naturally, this needs careful planning well in advance. Make sure you have agreed objectives as leaders so that the meeting, as well as being creative and lively, will also have a clear cutting edge in its message.

GOING UNDERGROUND

As you know, in some countries Christians have to meet secretly, like some of the early Christians in Rome. Have a secret meeting with your youth group. Arrange for a secret, coded message to pass between your members so that they are the only ones who know where and when the meeting is to take place.

Meet in a quiet spot – in a house, in the open, in shaded woodland, etc. Organize it so that your group arrives in pairs or singly, so as not to arouse suspicion.

Display, discreetly, the Christian sign of the fish. Sing quiet, worshipful songs. Have only one Bible, with your group offering memorized verses of the Bible. No books, guitars, etc.

As a finale read, or better still tell, the story of a real life secret church. You can obtain such stories from Eastern European organizations which advertise in the religious press. If your church permits it,

have a secret communion, involving some adult members of your congregation.

CHURCH OVER THERE

Get a couple of missionary organizations involved in different parts of the world to send you literature on churches in other countries. This will be greatly helped by the loan of slides, videos, etc, of overseas churches.

CHURCH AND ME

Plan to involve some of your young people in 'missions' organized by a reputable interdenominational body. Let them rub shoulders with other Christians in evangelism. But be careful – exposure to such activities will give you headaches when they get back. They will want to set your group and church on fire!

BLACK AND WHITE

The Christian church should, by definition, know no race barriers. But for a number of different reasons, you sometimes get a church with near total black or white membership.

If your church fits into that category you must arrange a visit to a predominantly black or white church even if it means travelling a fair distance. Arrange to meet socially with the congregation too.

The more exposure you give your group to Christians from other denominations and countries, the more you eradicate the breeding ground for petty church divisions and disharmony. Ignore it at your peril.

Bible study

With or without the vicar or minister, plan a Bible study on 'What is the church?'

- The church means a body of believers in all denominations, and not just a local congregation (Ephesians 2:19–22)
- The church traverses all racial barriers (Romans 10:11–13).
- The church includes poor and rich (James 1:9–11; 2:1–9).
- The church is world-wide (Paul's letter-writing to all nations).
- The church was founded by Christ (Matthew 16:18).
- The church in its early days was a community (Acts 2:42–47).
- The church is for different ages (Titus 2:2–8).
- The church is not perfect, eg the Corinthian church.
- The church in the New Testament was never described as a building, but as a body of true believers (1 Corinthians 1:2).
- The church is like a body whose parts are interdependent (1 Corinthians 12:12–31).

13 Meet the others!

You should be meeting youth groups or youth fellowships from other churches, but it is a bit boring to arrange to meet only in each others' meeting place at a set time. So try this with three church groups.

PREPARATION

Ask each leader to take two photographs of his group and send them, with a list of names corresponding to the photos, to the other groups two weeks before this meeting.

Pin the two you receive to the notice board so that the group begin to remember the faces and the names.

PROGRAMME

Group spotting

Arrange for this to take place in a very busy shopping precinct. In pairs, members of the groups make their way to the shopping area and mingle with the shoppers. They must ignore anyone they see from their own group. (This should not be done in the dark.)

When anyone sights somebody they recognize from the photos of other groups, they can go up to him or her and say, 'You are . . . and you go to . . . group.' If they are right (and hopefully they will be wrong a few times) they take the person/couple to the meeting place. This should not be too far away and should if possible be neutral, maybe someone's home.

Set a time to rendezvous, in case there are some who remain unidentified!

Back at the ranch

Your meeting should concentrate on your 'togetherness' and on what you agree about – not on the difference. FOOD is essential for this meeting.

Alternative

You could try any type of scavenger hunt alongside this exercise, or instead of it. Invite all the local youth fellowships to join you for it, and emphasize the fact that there will be food afterwards.

Try a **horrible scavenger hunt**. Send out in pairs all those who turn up, giving them a list of horrible things to collect.

13

For example:
- A cold chip.
- A piece of meat left over from a dog's dinner.
- A worm or snail (alive).
- A dead toothbrush with some toothpaste still on it.
- A used tea bag.
- A pair of false teeth.

Discussion

Jesus sent out the seventy (or seventy-two) in twos (Luke 10:1–16). A group discussion on the passage could be useful.

Discussion questions:
1. Why did Jesus say he was sending them out 'like lambs among wolves'?
2. Why were they encouraged not to take too much?
3. What was Jesus saying in verses 8–12 about the reaction to their message?
4. What does Jesus imply in verses 13–16 about our responsibility to deliver his message?
5. Put verse 16 in your own words.

14

Swopping hats

The 'pulpit exchange' is not something new. Most ministers give this a bash around Christian Unity Week and often enjoy going to another church to preach.

So why don't you?

PREPARATION

Arrange with your counterpart in St Cedd's to swop groups for one week . . . or permanently if you both enjoy it that much! *You* stay in your normal meeting place, and let the *groups* swop over. They will discover where the other one meets, whether the chairs are comfortable or not, what sort of records/CDs/videos the other leader has and whether he or she can make decent coffee.

Check with your church leaders before doing this as it may give rise to some 'political' difficulties of which you are unaware.

Agree on a subject to tackle and on how you are going to develop it. It is best to use the same subject. A helpful and relevant one would be, 'What is the church?' The study below will get you started.

Romans 12:5
1 Corinthians 12:27–28
Ephesians 1:22–23; 4:11–12
Colossians 1:24; 2:19

Follow-up

The following week, return to your own group and share your discoveries of the previous week.

As well as meeting with the other leader prior to this event you will need to do so afterwards to discuss how things went. Hopefully you will find time to pray together and to develop other opportunities to work together again in the future.

SUGGESTED STUDY

The body of Christ

Each group should create a 'cooking' recipe for the ideal church. They do this by listing all the 'ingredients' from the references below, then adding quantities and cooking instructions. Then compare recipes.

The vicar under the light

What is your vicar or church leader like?

If he is secure in his position invite him to meet your group!

PREPARATION

Make sure that he understands your aims and what is expected of him: he will be put under the spotlight (literally) and asked to answer any question the youth group may throw in his direction. It could be on church politics, the Bible, the leader's personal walk with God; no holds barred.

PROGRAMME

This needs a leader who feels he can cope with your group, and you will need to protect him a little if you feel the questions are way off beam. The blame for things going wrong must always land on you rather than on the invited guest.

The only rule is that the leader may at any time, without any further comment, 'pass' a question. If your group are slow at coming forward it may be better to get them to write their questions down beforehand. On the night, the guest takes them out of a hat to read and answer them.

If your church has a leadership team, ask the lot along to face the group together.

Alternative

Another time reverse and extend the roles. Have some members of your youth group under the spotlight, with selected church members asking them questions. Set up good spotlights to set the scene.

If people are honest, both exercises can be very helpful. In the second one you may find out more about your young people than you ever knew before, and the church leader will hopefully gain an insight into the thoughts and feelings of the teenagers he preaches to each Sunday. If the leader is honest in the first round, the group could find that a lot of their fears and misconceptions about Christianity vanish. Precisely the opposite, of course, could happen . . . which is why you need to think about that first question, 'What is your vicar like?'!

16 Get the lads round!

What happens when people miss your meetings and you want to add a little bit of subtle pressure to get them back?
Easily solved: send the lads round.

PREPARATION

Announce the week before: 'If you do not turn up next week and have not given a legitimate excuse then we are all going to turn up on your doorstep!'

Whether you can do this or not of course depends on how seriously they take your threat! This is something you will have to decide to do on the spot when you find that someone has not turned up to a meeting. It is great fun for a 'once-off' so that people can let off steam; the end of the exam season is a good time to try it.

Be sensitive to your young people's domestic situation. But really beef it up if you know the parents well – invade them! It is a nice way to make friends.

PROGRAMME

The New Testament uses a special word for fellowship – *koinonia* in Greek – and you may wish to do a word study on it once you have arrived at the person's house.

The verses below give various examples of what it means to have 'fellowship' with God and each other. Ask the group to get into twos or threes and to list the ways in which fellowship differs from friendship.

- 1 Corinthians 1:9
- 2 Corinthians 8:3–4 ('sharing' in verse 4 is the way *koinonia* or 'fellowship' has been translated)
- Galatians 2:9
- Philippians 1:3–5 (*koinonia* has been translated as 'partnership')
- Philippians 2:1; 3:10
- 1 John 1:3, 6–7

Thanks!!

17

I am not one for traditions unless they are good ones. One of the saddest obituaries is, 'We've always done it this way.'

But saying 'thanks' is one of those traditions which Jesus himself taught us (see the story of the one leper out of the ten healed who returned to say, 'thanks', Luke 17:11–19).

We need to be thankful, so let's start with the small things and build up to bigger ones.

PROGRAMME

Songs and discussion

1 Sing a few thankful songs to begin with. If you have never sung before as a group perhaps this is the time to try.

2 Throw a stack of newspapers on the floor and ask your group to find and tear out two stories which reflect an element of appreciation and thanks. This may be difficult – which will be a message in itself. Ask two different people to read out the stories, or give summaries of them.

3 Turn to Luke 17:11–19 (have photocopies of the passage available), and have it read 'dramatically' – with someone being the narrator, another taking the part of Jesus and another two or three to be lepers.

Ask the group afterwards why they think the other nine did not return. Keep the discussion brief.

Thank you lists

Hand out some pieces of paper, one for each person, and ask everyone to put their names on the top. They should then write down two or three things about themselves for which they are thankful: good health, parents etc. If the group know each other reasonably well, collect up the papers and then hand them out again, making sure that no one gets their own paper back. When everyone has someone else's sheet each person should place himself or herself in the shoes of the person whose paper he or she has, and should ask himself, 'If I were this person, what would I be grateful for?' The list can be as long as they wish, provided it is genuine . . . they can each give reasons if they like. Then the paper should be passed back to the owner for viewing. The degree of discussion and interaction which follow will depend on how well group members know each other.

Thank you notelets

Two 'thank you' notelets should be handed to each person. On one they should write a thank you note to someone who has helped them in the past but who they have never really thanked properly. It could be a Sunday school teacher, minister, teacher, friend etc. Give them an envelope to put it in and offer a postage stamp to anyone who will need to post theirs.

Inside the other 'thank you' notelet they should write 'Dear God', and follow that with a letter of thanks. Their thanks should be totally sincere, but can be for anything. Some of these could then be read out as prayers. They could also be read out, as an offering of thanks, at church on Sunday as part of the 'family worship'. If yours is an Anglican church you could suggest to the vicar that they are read before Communion and then laid on the altar.

Reading out of these thanks can be very meaningful and should not be glossed over. Allow a few seconds' silence after each 'thank you' has been read out. Finally, after the thank you notelets/prayers, read Psalm 136:1–9 together, the 'classic' when it comes to 'thank you' psalms. You read the first line and ask the group to say the response together, 'His love endures for ever'.

17

17

Option

If you are a very 'rich' group, hand out 50p in bright shiny coins from the bank (have a word with your local bank manager), and ask each person to buy a gift for someone else this week. It need not be someone in the group. They are to give it to the person, without the person knowing who it is from. All it should say with it is, 'Thank you.'

Thank you for getting this far!

Here is a crazy idea that will probably work if you show that you are both enthusiastic and serious.

PREPARATION

Instead of letting the young people attend the youth meeting, tell them to stay at home and to send their parents instead.

You will need to back this up with enthusiastic personal invitations to the parents, such as a telephone call or personal visit, saying that it is essential that they come. 'All the other parents are coming and it would be sad if you missed out!'

PROGRAMME

What do you do? Simple! You just 'do' a normal youth meeting so that they can see what you do and how you do it. Do not change anything other than outrageously boisterous activities.

Most parents will be very glad to have the chance to see what really goes on, and the evening may well open up opportunities for your involvement with the parents at a much deeper level.

Please treat everyone the same, whether they are committed Christians or not, but be careful how you handle your questions and who you ask.

THOSE OUT THERE

Evangelism usually means us Christians telling non-Christians what we think.

But a vital part of bringing the Good News to the young unchurched is to find out what *they* think – about life, about work, about politics, about the church.

Unless we come into regular contact with young people we will not know where their needs lie and how the gospel might best be presented to them.

This session helps you prepare for evangelism among young non-Christians and it involves tape recording, and word association games.

PREPARATION

Ask two or three members of your group to let you meet their non-Christian friends. Let them arrange the venue, anywhere they like.

Tell them you are wanting to get their views and ideas on a variety of topics and you want to record the conversations, but with no names.

Take someone with you to work the tape recorder but scrap it and take notes if you find the tape recorder is making people feel self-conscious. Usually these discussions are so fascinating you will remember what has been said.

PROGRAMME

Meet young people

Having met up with the young people, bought coffees and told them about yourself, tell them you are going to give them one topic at a time and you want them to react by giving you their views on that subject (see list of subjects in box). Record their comments.

Control group

Organize the same exercise with your own youth group and record their reactions.

Edit the tape of your meeting with the non-Christians picking out the best comments. This does not have to be professional, simply use two tape recorders and record from one to the other.

Play the tape to your group and ask for their reactions. Try to draw out the differences in the responses from the Christian and the non-Christian group (if there are any).

Draw together any biblical comments on the subjects which have been discussed but only if they are relevant to the topic. (See biblical references in box. Make sure you read them carefully first to get the full picture.)

19

Topics

Death
Work/Unemployment
God
Marriage/Sex
School
Jesus
The Law
Mrs Thatcher
Church
Violence

Parents, church leaders and members

Do not leave this bit out; it could be the most exciting part of the exercise.

Invite your church leaders and any interested church members to meet up with your youth group for an evening's discussion.

Play the tapes of your youth group and their non-Christian peers. If you are clever with a camera, you may also show slide photographs of young people to correspond with the tape recordings. It would be even better if you could prepare and play a tape of older members of the church talking on the same topics.

Lead an interesting debate on one or two of the topics raised in your talks with young people, either in small groups or all together.

The aim of the debate should be:

● To draw up a programme for the church to tackle some of the issues raised by young non-Christians.
● To work out ways in which evangelism can be made relevant to young people outside the church.

BIBLE REFERENCES	
Death	● Hebrews 9:27–28 ● Genesis 2:15–17
Work/Unemployment	● 2 Thessalonians 3:6–8 ● 1 Timothy 5:8 ● Ecclesiastes 2:17–25
God	● Genesis 1:1 ● Acts 14:15; 17:24–28 ● Psalm 103:1–19 ● Psalm 139:1–16 ● Amos 2:6–8 ● Luke 15:11–23
Marriage/Sex	● Genesis 2:19–24 ● 1 Corinthians 13:4–7 ● 1 Corinthians 6:12–20 ● Ephesians 5:22–23
School	● Proverbs 13:1 ● 1 Peter 2:13–17
Jesus	● John 10:30; 14:23; 14:9; 8:46 ● Matthew 11:29 ● John 17:4–5 ● Matthew 12:6,32 ● John 14:6
The Law	● Matthew 17:24–27; 22:15–22 ● Acts 5:29 ● Romans 13:1–7
Mrs Thatcher	● Philippians 1:27 ● 1 Peter 2:13–17
Church	● Matthew 16:16–18 ● John 1:12 ● Ephesians 2:19–22 ● 1 Corinthians 12:12–13
Violence	● James 4:1–3 ● John 8:3–11

Getting on the air waves

The local radio station has given your youth group five five-minute 'Thought for the day' slots. They are to be on a 'popular' station which usually presents pop music, and your slots will go out in between the chart tracks. 'Now's my chance!' you think to yourself. 'I'll preach the gospel ... they won't stand a chance by the time I've finished with them!'

But *what* are you going to say and *how* would you put together a series which expresses the Christian faith?

To get your group thinking through this assignment seriously, run it over two weeks or take a whole day for it.

The reason for getting your youth group to do this, is that they will learn more from *doing* a presentation of the Christian faith than from simply *reading* about it. They will have to know their material very well to present it. This may sound sly, but we are called to be 'as shrewd as snakes and as innocent as doves' (Matthew 10:16)!

PREPARATION

1 Listen to some 'Thoughts for the day' on various radio stations to get an idea how it is done ... that is, before you decide how to improve them.

2 Listen to some pop radio stations to get an idea of the ethos behind some top-of-the-chart shows so that you can slot in.

3 Telephone your local radio station and speak to the head of religious broadcasting. Ask his advice on what makes a good 'thought for the day' slot, and tell him what you are doing. He might be willing to come and speak to your youth group one evening before you prepare your 'slots'. And you never know, he might like the idea so much that he will agree to broadcast one or more of your programmes – though probably with some revision.

4 Plan well . . . so that the second or third week you have the necessary recording equipment (and silence). There is always someone who has the equipment – local hi-fi shop, even the radio station – and who will let you borrow it, particularly if you indicate that you are also inviting 'the press' to come to take some pictures and write a story.

Points to remember
- God slots are the breaks that are expected to be boring.
- Five minutes is all you get.
- Your opening sentence 'grabs' or 'loses' your listeners.
- Your final statement should summarize your content, should be pithy and should leave the listener space to think further.

And now Thought for Breakfastime from the Very Reverend Julian Pendletwistle, Prebendary of the Diocese of Greater Piddle...

How **not** to do it ...

20

PROGRAMME

Suggested theme

What better theme to use as the base for your message than the early apostolic preaching of the gospel? (cf 1 Corinthians 1:21). Now in your broadcast you obviously don't use these terms but in essence I would suggest the following thematic approach for your five broadcasts:

ONE

The prophets of old had foretold this event: Jesus' ministry, death and resurrection.

Emphasis:

This amazing event had been foretold many hundreds of years before.

Verses for study:

Acts 2:16; 3:18, 24

TWO

Because of the resurrection, Jesus has taken his special place with God.

Emphasis:

The resurrection was such an amazing event that it showed the world that Jesus IS the Son of God.

Verses:

Acts 2.33–36; 3.13; 4.11; 5.31.

THREE

The Holy Spirit in the church is the true sign of Christ's presence and power.

Emphasis:

Christ has left us with his presence.

Verses:

Acts 2.17–21, 33; 5.32.

FOUR

Christ will one day return at the end of the age.

Emphasis:

Christ has left us for a while but will return to 'call' those who have believed to his new kingdom.

Verses:

Acts 3.20; 10.42.

FIVE

It is necessary to repent, to receive forgiveness and the assistance of the Holy Spirit.

Emphasis:

Eternity begins now for those who find true forgiveness through repentance and the life of Christ through the Holy Spirit.

Verses:

Acts 2.38; 3.19, 25; 4.12; 5.31; 10.43

Important

Your programmes should be simple . . . **KISS—Keep It Simple, Stupid!** They should be making just one major point . . . what is it? Personal testimony is important. Variety (not too much) is essential.

For my interest please send scripts to me via Scripture Union, 130 City Road, London EC1V 2NJ.

Apologetics

'Stone an atheist' is often the attitude we have when trying to argue for the truth of Christianity against the vigorous denial of it by an atheist or agnostic.

'Apologetics' is the art of giving clear, objective reasons for what we believe – being able to answer for 'the hope that is within us' as the Bible puts it.

But what normally happens when a Christian and an atheist or agnostic confront each other is that they spend hours locked in meaningless discussion. The two square up, launch their hail of word missiles at each other and then walk off, each thinking he has won.

Christians normally take one of two stands in the great apologetics battle. Some say you only have to live out the Christian life in practice for others to see that it is true. Others would argue that, as Christians, we should have all the answers to beat over the head of the miserable sinner who refuses to believe. In this section we are going to explore the middle path. It is called 'diplomacy'.

PROGRAMME

During about twenty minutes the atheists should argue their views. Suggest to them in advance that they might like to include the problems and accusations shown in the 'Stone a Christian' box. Encourage them to be aggressive in their arguments.

Stone an atheist

Now allow your group to tackle the atheists. Give them at least twenty minutes to do this and make sure that no one person hogs the dialogue.

Then come clean

Give your atheists another few minutes to refute their own previous atheistic views. They should be encouraged to use the Bible, common sense, historical and scientific data where necessary.

Do not say anything to your group about this, just give a quiet, unobtrusive signal for your atheists to become Christians again. Watch the reactions of your group.

PREPARATION

Hire an atheist

Arrange for two or three Christians to become atheists for an evening. They should be unknown to your young people. Contact a local or not-so-local church to find suitable candidates to play atheists. They must be good thinkers and be able to present their case.

STONE A CHRISTIAN

1 Hypocrisy of church members; all they are really interested in is money and buildings.
2 The church has been involved in wars, brutality and torture throughout the centuries.
3 Problems of pain and suffering in the world.
4 Problems of evil in the world – a loving God? Who are you kidding?
5 Don't all religions lead to God anyway?
6 No one has seen God.

21

Reaction time

Split your group into smaller units for easier discussion and give them time to answer the questions in the 'Stone Me!' box.

Burying stone

As a leader, you will discover that this session has opened up a number of issues which will need answering. You may worry that what you appear to have done is to sow 'doubts' in the minds of your young people. Probably many of these were already there.

Make sure your atheists do a good job when they become Christians again so that your group may be aware that there are answers to criticism. It would be wrong to say that there are answers to all atheistic comments and questions.

In the end, our belief is not based on having all the facts but on a faith in Jesus Christ which is based on adequate evidence.

STONE ME!

1 What was your attitude towards the atheists when you could not answer their arguments?
2 Did you feel very frustrated at not being able to give an adequate answer to the problems raised?
3 Was there any truth in their comments? If so, how did you feel about it? Can you do anything to change the situation?
4 What can we do to be more equipped to answer some of the issues raised by our atheist friends?
5 The 'hypocrisy' in the church – is it real?

Faith has three parts:

- **Belief** – in facts (known) supported by evidence
- **Trust** – confidence in the object of faith
- **Action** – personal involvement

Belief is based on examination of the evidence. Your investigation of the evidence leads you to a rational decision to agree with the facts. Suppose that someone says that a certain aeroplane is safe. The flight record of the plane (evidence) verifies the information. So you decide to believe the facts (John 20:31 and John 1:12).

Trust is based on personal confidence in the object of your belief. This act of your will says 'I believe in the facts which say the plane can carry me. Therefore, I trust it.' The evidence has proved the object of your faith is valid, so you exercise personal confidence in it (John 1:12).

Action takes personal involvement. You pin all your hopes on something and relax. That would involve boarding the plane and letting it carry you to your destination (John 1:12).

BECOMING MORE
LIKE CHRIST

Dealing with anger 22

'You brainless idiot! You stupid, half-witted fool!'
Have you ever muttered such sentiments under your breath while your nostrils flame with fire?
Do you ever get home on the point of explosion wishing you had told someone exactly what you think of their pious, bombastic, arrogant attitude?

If you have not, then you are either out of touch with your emotions or you are lying to yourself. Everyone gets angry at some point, so we are going to look at this violent emotion and how to deal with it.

PREPARATION

Set up an explosive, angry incident. Arrange beforehand with a fellow youth worker or the owner of the house in which you meet that you will knock over and smash a vase or some other object and that he or she will then come and explode with anger and rage at the breakage.

PROGRAMME

Act it out

Do this during the preliminaries of your meeting. Practise beforehand if necessary and do not go on for longer than a minute before the angry person walks out in disgust. Your response to the angry blow-up should be passive: play it down, telling the youth group you will sort it out later.

Talk about it

Admit it was a mocked-up stunt, or have your actor/actress walk in again immediately and with a big smile ask, 'How did I do then?'
Then get your group to discuss what went on. Discussion should cover the following:

● Was the house owner justified in expressing his anger?
● Did the youth leader react rightly?
● Did the youth leader's passive attitude help?
● How did the group feel while it was all happening?
● How do they feel when they have been angry with someone close to them?

Discuss it

Promote further discussion by getting your group to complete the 'Anger quiz'.
Complete the quiz yourself and then lead a discussion on the results.

Understand it

Read Matthew 5:21–26 to your group and share some thoughts on Jesus' teaching on anger, based on the notes below:

● **Sometimes it's right to be angry.** We should be rightly angry at some things that happen. Angry at the starvation in the world, angry at abuse of children and adults; angry at abuse of power; angry at terrorism.
Jesus was angry with the merchants in the temple who were making a profit out of people's devotion to God.
Martin Luther talks about this type of anger as the anger of love – one that is friendly to the person but hostile to the sin.

● **Revenge only backfires on you (v 22).** The anger Jesus talks of here is the one which never forgets what someone did to you.
Such anger only harms you. It twists the mind and makes you feel bitter. Life begins to get out of perspective.

● **Anger leads to insults (v 22).** Jesus denounces anger which leads to insults. The word 'raca' is Aramaic and its meaning is obscure, but the nearest translation is 'empty-headed, brainless idiot, you're not worth my spit as I walk past you'. This is anger at its ugliest.

22

- **Anger destroys reputations (v 22).** When you are so inflamed with anger that you start to tell people exactly how you feel about them you cannot reverse the process. You have damaged their reputation and even if you apologize you cannot stop the negative gossip you have initiated. To get this idea across, squeeze some toothpaste into a bowl and then ask someone to put it back in the tube!

- **God loves the people who anger you.** Your reaction to someone who makes you angry shows how you value them. When we feel anger we should ask ourselves, 'What value does this person have in the eyes of the Creator?' It has been said 'If there is no God, there is no meaning, if there is no meaning, there is no value, if there is no value, you're worth nothing.' The principle here is: **Don't step on toes while you're washing feet.'**

ANGER QUIZ

Tick the statements with which you agree.

1 Anger is a means of getting something off your chest.

2 Christians should never demonstrate anger.

3 God-given anger is meant to be used constructively.

4 Anger should be expressed immediately.

5 I should never show anger – I should gradually let off steam in private.

6 Some world disasters and diseases are God's way of showing anger.

7 You can have a 'right' anger about something.

8 Controlled anger shown by parents to their children is an essential means of discipline.

9 If people would learn how to argue properly they would not get so angry.

10 Everybody gets angry.

11 If you are angry it is best to do some physical exercise to work it off.

12 You should never suppress anger.

DISPLEASED   ANNOYED   ANGRY   ENRAGED   HOMICIDAL

You'd better! Or else!

Psychiatrists are inundated with people who feel guilty. Frequently this has stemmed from their wrong use of anger. Anger is one of those powerful emotions which often catches us out ... we try to keep cool but it suddenly takes us over and we find ourselves expressing words and sentiments which we later regret.

Then there are those of us, of whom I am one (I think), who let anger simmer inside and try not to let it show *too* much . . . but just enough for the other person to know what we are feeling!!!

Jesus showed anger in the temple so maybe it is all right to be angry; but when? Use this outline to help your group explore this highly charged area.

PREPARATION

There are two ways in which you could set the scene:

1 Arrange for two people in your group to have an argument near the beginning of the meeting, starting small but becoming increasingly aggressive. Make sure that when you intervene to stop them, one of them pushes you away and tells you to 'clear off'. Allow time for people to 'feel' the emotions of the scene. Then, after a few more moments, announce that the subject under discussion tonight is anger!

2 Arrange for one member of your group to go out on the streets with a cassette recorder to interview passers-by, asking them:

● What kind of things make you angry?
● How do you express your anger?
● What do you do to try to stop losing your temper?
● After you have been angry and lost your cool, how do you feel?

Arrange for some editing work to be done on the tape before playing. This is quite simple if you use a two-tape deck. Keep the comments flowing.

PROGRAMME

Setting the scene

Start off either with the angry scene above, or by playing the editorial tape.

A case in point

Hand out photocopies of the Peter and Daniel 'situation' below and, in groups of four or five, have group members discuss this with the aid of the questions. After seventeen minutes bring them back into the larger group for feedback.

Daniel and Peter

Daniel and Peter are at college. They are usually good friends and share a room in a house near the college. One evening Peter comes back to discover that Daniel has invited a group of friends over and had forgotten to tell him. Peter was intending to get on quietly with an essay which he had to have finished by the next day. He had deliberately left college to get away from 'friends' so that he could get on with his work.

When Peter sees what is happening he is really angry. Without saying anything he storms out of the house, slamming the door.

Two hours later he returns and has a blazing row with Daniel. Daniel apologizes profusely for not notifying him but, 'it had been one of those spontaneous meetings of friends'. Daniel did not lose his cool and refused to be drawn into exchanging insults. This made things worse because Peter tried to provoke him, wanting an excuse to shout even more loudly.

Next morning, Peter ate breakfast without speaking to Daniel, and walked off to college by himself.

23

Questions

1 Why do we feel anger? What is it inside us that causes us to feel as Peter did?

2 Anger produces physiological changes in us (has a bodily effect). How does anger affect you physically?

3 How would you define the emotion of anger?

4 Why did Peter get even more angry when Daniel refused to argue back?

5 Was Peter right to express his feelings in this way or should he have kept his feelings to himself?

6 If you had been Peter how would you have reacted?

Discussion

Ask two people to read the two different Bible passages below. Then discuss the implications of the stories with the total group. It is best to have the same version of the Bible for the whole group.

Anger in the Bible

Read the temple story (John 2:13–17).

● What emotion do you think Jesus was expressing? How right do you think he was to feel this way and to do what he did?

Read Ephesians 4:26–27.

● How can we be angry and not sin? What are these verses saying to us? If you can, give an example from your own experience of a time when you did what verse 26 advises, and another example of a time when 'the devil got a foothold' (v 27).

Share the guidelines below with the group, using your own experience, as well as that of others in the group (with their permission) to give concrete examples.

At the end you may feel it appropriate to have a time of silent or audible confession.

GUIDELINES

1 Anger is something which is common to us all, but different personalities express it in different ways. Some express their feelings very demonstratively: everybody hears about it! Others allow their anger to smoulder inside. Both expressions of anger can be bad, but the person who lets it smoulder normally suffers more.

2 Anger can be right if it is expressed against injustice or if, in Luther's words, it 'is friendly to the person but hostile to sin'. Making this sort of distinction is something which most of us find very difficult.

3 Anger is a powerful emotion which can destroy us. It is one which, if left unchecked, can make us very bitter.

4 Anger needs to be tackled carefully and consciously:
● Always deal quickly with the consequences of your anger.
● Review your progress daily without getting paranoid.
● Admit it if you have done wrong (1 John 1:9).
● Remember that God has promised to help you (1 Corinthians 10:13).
● When something makes you angry, remember that you can choose how to respond – you do not have to flip your lid!

Dealing with guilt

24

Lady Macbeth is found frantically washing her blood-stained hands late at night, trying to wash away her guilt.

Peter takes tablets four times a day to dull the feelings of guilt that have ravaged his body and mind for a number of years.

Joan cannot cope at all with what she knows about herself; she takes the only way out that she knows and deals with it once and for all.

Guilt is not a modern problem; it began with Eve and Adam in the garden of Eden when they felt 'ashamed' and hid themselves from God. Modern psychiatry, which brings it all to the surface and leaves it there, cannot give adequate therapy to the guilt-ridden person.

Here is an exercise which is important in helping young people to think through this subject. Three things are *vital* for success of this meeting: Your **preparation**, your **honesty**, your **specific prayers for each member of your group**; they may want to respond at a very deep level to this session.

PREPARATION

Consider specific areas of your life where guilt seemed to play an important role when you were young.

Review the following material very carefully so that you are quite clear about what is required.

Prepare a photocopy of the discussion questions below and of 'Steps to take'.

PROGRAMME

Discussion 1

In groups of four or six discuss these questions:

1 What causes a person to feel guilty?
2 What is guilt, anyway?

3 What part does God play in our feelings of guilt? Please give a couple of real life examples.
4 Is guilt ever inspired by the devil?
5 If someone does not feel guilty, does that mean he or she is not actually guilty? Again, give some examples.

Here are some of the things that you should draw out of the questions above. The numbers below relate to the numbers of the questions:

1 A person's violation of his own inner code of conduct – the standards he sets for himself and tries to live up to. Those standards might be ones given by God, or they might be ones that other people or the person himself impose on him.

2 A message of disapproval from your inner self (conscience) which says, 'you should be ashamed of yourself!'

3 God has given us 'codes of conduct' in the Old and New Testaments. If we do not keep these we *should* feel guilty. Feeling guilty in this case is a good thing because it shows we are aware of our sin.

However, in the death of Jesus God has provided a way for us to be completely blameless in his sight. Though we will still break God's 'codes of conduct' from day to day, we can ask for his forgiveness because Jesus has already taken our punishment.

4 Yes. He tells you that you cannot be forgiven or that you are too bad to be forgiven. And he adds, 'So you might as well carry on with what you're doing.'

He also puts thoughts into our minds like, 'God won't really mind; and anyway, he'll forgive you.' So we go ahead and do what we know is wrong, but have let ourselves be persuaded is all right really. Then the devil looks over our shoulder and says, 'You've done it once; you might as well do it again.' And then that wrong action can become a habit.

The devil also accuses us falsely of doing wrong, in the hope that we will feel we are too bad for God to accept us.

5 No. Many characters in history and in our newspapers have gone to their graves without any apparent remorse, eg Hitler, Stalin.

Discussion 2

Now move the discussion on to tackle this problem:

How do feelings of guilt relate to our consciences? Do we know whether we are really guilty of sin or not?

Ask the group to look up these references to **conscience**, and to say how it is described. Points to draw out are given in brackets:

CONSCIENCE

- 1 Corinthians 8:7   (It can be weak; not sure what is genuinely right or wrong.)

- Titus 1:15   (It can be corrupted so that it no longer bothers a person when he or she does wrong.)

- 1 Timothy 3:9   (It can be kept pure.)

- Acts 23:1   (It can assure someone that he or she has done the right thing.)

- Romans 2:15   (It can indicate what is right and what is wrong.)

Add the following three points:

1 The Holy Spirit sharpens our conscience when we become Christians, so that we are more aware of what is right and wrong.
2 Habits begin as 'cobwebs' – they are easy to break out of; but if they are allowed to continue they become 'cables' which bind and trap us.
3 We cannot always trust our conscience. Experiences we have had and choices we have made can distort its sense of right and wrong.

Explain to the group that because our consciences cannot always be trusted we are going to have to find out how to test them. To answer the question, 'Is my conscience telling the truth?' we need to go through various 'government departments'. Each department will give us something by which to test our conscience's decision:

STEP ONE:

Go to **THE DEPARTMENT OF EMOTIONS**. You might be *feeling* guilty, but beware! Emotions are not always right. An emotion is your reaction to a situation as you understand it – *you might have understood it wrongly*. For example, young children whose parents split up often feel guilty because they think it is their fault. But they have understood the situation wrongly; the splitting up is not their fault and they should not feel guilty.

So have you understood the situation? Move on to step two to find out.

STEP TWO:

Go to **THE DEPARTMENT OF MORALS**. Your morals are what you think right and wrong are. What you find in this department will depend on what you have fed into it in the past. You might have some biblical standards of right and wrong; you might have taken on some of the moral standards of your parents; you might have added to these or altered them with other ideas of right and wrong which you have picked up from what you have read, or seen on TV.

This department is subject to error; it will give you a quick summary of your moral standards but you still can't be sure that these are the right standards. So move on to step three.

STEP THREE:

Go to **THE DEPARTMENT OF KNOWLEDGE AND REASON**. This department will give you the rational criteria for your thinking. It will tell you what God's standards are by checking out the principles he gives in the Bible. People you will find working in this department are pastors and Bible teachers, authors of helpful Christian books, and wise Christian friends. All these will be able to help you test your own standards against those of God's to ascertain whether or not you should be feeling guilty.

STEP FOUR:

Go to **THE DEPARTMENT OF THE WILL**. This is where you are left on your own to decide your course of action. All the other departments have helped you find out what is right; now you know, you must decide what to do about it. Through the 'steps' you may have discovered that you are not guilty; God does not condemn you. So you now have to make up your mind as to whether you will receive the releasing verdict of 'Not guilty'.

The 'steps' may have shown you that your feeling of guilt was right. In which case you will need to confess your sin to God, then ask for and accept his forgiveness in order for that guilt emotion to be erased.

End by reading 1 John 1:5–10. Allow the group to remain in quiet or open prayer for a few minutes.

25

Jigsaw him!

Other people determine your actions and thoughts. 'Not I!' you say, probably with some justification, but only **some**. We are constantly influenced by others: parents, friends, television, magazines, the Bible.

not forget to delegate; that is, ask some of your non-involved older church members to help. Explain what the jigsaws are for so that they can also pray for you more intelligently on the night.

For each nine-piece jigsaw take one photo and stick it on to the centre piece of the jigsaw. Place all the pieces into an envelope, with a felt-tip pen, and write the person's name on the outside.

PROGRAMME

On the evening give each person their jigsaw and ask them to make it up – make it a race.

Now ask them to write, on each

of the pieces around the picture, one thing which affects and influences them. Use some of the examples above to stimulate their thinking, eg 'friends'. On the reverse of the jigsaw they are to be more specific about these influences. For example, 'Bill and Tom get me into trouble'. Or, 'John is a good influence on me because. . .' Next to each specific example of the influences, they should put a plus or minus sign, depending on whether that specific influence is positive (plus) or negative (minus).

Read Romans 12:1–2 and 1 Corinthians 10:13 to the group and ask them to sketch another jigsaw which shows the people and things they would prefer to influence them. Finally, they should pass their jigsaws to you. Pray for each 'new' person (jigsaw) in turn then return the jigsaws to the group members.

PREPARATION

The week before your meeting, obtain a small passport photograph of each member of your group. You could even set up a quick photography session during refreshments the previous week and have a 'friend' come and take a mug shot of each person. Make sure that if someone is missing you arrange to collect a photograph of them during the week. Of course, do not tell them what you want it for . . . they come along to find out!

Buy some card and make a number of nine-piece jigsaws, one for each member of your group. Do

Back to the graph paper

We are going to look at ourselves 'holistically' in this session. That is, as people who are not simply 'souls' walking around on two feet, but whose spiritual, physical, mental and social aspects are closely bound up together.

PREPARATION

Buy some graph paper and enough felt-tip pens or coloured pencils for each person in your group to have four different colours.

Ask them to draw the two axes of a graph. On the vertical side they should mark off numbers 1 to 10 and on the horizontal line they should list the last twelve months (all, of course, with regular spacing). It may be easier for you to do this in advance and give each person a photocopy. The graph should be titled **Growth over the last year** (see example below).

PROGRAMME

Growth charts

Using a different colour of pen for each category, members of the group should estimate on a scale of one to ten how much, over the year, they have developed:

- physically: allow for a few giggles and laughs;
- mentally: how they are developing in their studies;
- socially: how well they are developing friendships with people of both sexes;
- spiritually: how they are developing and becoming stronger as Christians.

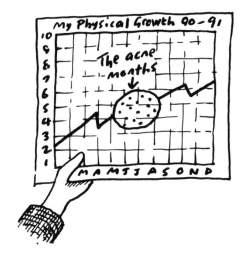

The graph will give them an instant visual idea of how they think they are doing.

Important: Do tell them that what they think about their own growth may not necessarily be what others think. In adolescence we tend to 'put ourselves down'.

You may wish to go over some verses on spiritual growth with the group (see below). You may also want to let them know that you are with anyone who wishes to talk over matters which concern them. However, beware of creating problems for yourself if you give confidential counsel to someone of the opposite sex.

Spiritual growth

Put your young people into small groups and give them the following verses to look up. With the graph in mind, they should make a list of all the areas of spiritual growth mentioned.

Then each person should list, on their own, the goals they are going to aim for this year.

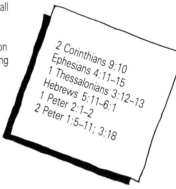

2 Corinthians 9:10
Ephesians 4:11–15
1 Thessalonians 3:12–13
Hebrews 5:11–6:1
1 Peter 2:1–2
2 Peter 1:5–11; 3:18

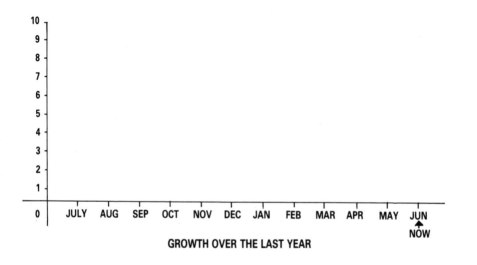

GROWTH OVER THE LAST YEAR

Gutsy Christianity

27

A few years ago, *Buzz* magazine (now *21st Century Christian*) ran an article which caused a big fuss and drew an enormous postbag. Was it an attack on the shepherding movement? Was it a critique of prosperity teaching? No, it was, 'Why Are Christian Men Wet?'

Evangelist Eric Delve wrote a blistering attack on the weak, the wet and the wimpy, and even the weediest of male readers managed to lift a pen and write in with their views.

But do we now have that gutsy Christianity Eric Delve was pleading for? The fact that so many Christian ministries today are aimed at shaking young Christians out of their complacency suggests we do not. Perhaps it is not always young people's fault, so this session is dedicated to making Christianity tough.

PROGRAMME

Hunky Hike

Arrange a hike for your youth group – not a Saturday stroll but a real muscle-straining incident-packed experience. Here are some suggestions:

- Get some people to carry 60lb rucksacks.

- Give out basic rations. Each person gets three ounces of muesli-mix in a plastic bag. No utensils allowed. Drinking water has to be poured into the plastic bag and drunk out of that.

- Organize the route so that it goes through muck, mud and streams.

- Get parents, scouts or cadets to mock up an incident which your group has to deal with on the way, eg, getting someone across a stream with only four large plastic bags, six poles and some rope.

- Ask the Red Cross or St John's Ambulance to stunt up an 'injured' person en route. The group gets a demonstration of how to put on a splint, for example, then they have to do it themselves.

- Blindfold the whole team and have them follow a rope through trees, bushes and man-made obstructions.

27

Base camp

When they get back to base camp they will be ready to die or kill you off or both. Feed them well with camp-style food and a few little extras to show you appreciate them.

Important

Safety is your number one concern. Do not try any of the above ideas without qualified leaders and adapt the route to suit the age and abilities of your group. It might be best to split people into teams with even muscle power and intellectual power.

As the teams meet with each incident or challenge, have someone watch their performance and give them points for team spirit, endurance, etc.

Post mortem

Keep it light, but get a discussion going about team spirit and meeting challenges:

Gutsy and growing

Using James 1:2–4 and Romans 5:3–5, outline the importance of hardship and testing to growth as a Christian and as a whole.

You could ask members of the team to act out the concepts listed in these verses, showing situations in which these characteristics are crucial to success.

For instance, for 'endurance' use the idea of running a race even when you feel like giving up.

Explain that the tests and trials we face produce patience and perseverance which is gradually building our characters. All our yesterdays are preparing us for all our tomorrows. God gives us certain tasks depending on our maturity to cope with them. See 2 Corinthians 1:12–14.

Use events which have occurred during the day to illustrate your talk.

This session is a great team builder and can influence your young people's futures quite significantly. Seek out summer opportunities such as evangelism, camps, etc in which they can be involved and which will stretch them and broaden their horizons.

- What were the most difficult things to handle on the course and why?
- Did every member of the team get on with the others throughout the course? What relationship problems were there? (No names!)
- What differences did good or bad team relations make to the success of the day?

Leadership

This meeting is designed to introduce 'leadership' to your young people, the leaders of tomorrow ... or even of today. An additional bonus is that it will give you the chance to compare your own leadership qualities with those listed in the Bible!

You will have one of two reactions to this meeting: 'No, I can't do this' or 'Yes, I will do this in spite of my insecurity, because I want to learn from my young people.'
To set yourself up as a leader means that you have already agreed to be open to criticism, so play dangerously and give this a go.

PROGRAMME

Arrival

When your group arrives have nothing arranged – no chairs, no refreshments, no props.
Watch to see if anybody attempts to organize the furniture or people. Of necessity your meeting will start late. (This is what usually happens anyway, you **must** take on this session for your own sake!)

What can we do?

Announce that you are not sure what to do for the meeting. Ask them to get into groups (let them decide which) and discuss what everyone could do for the rest of the evening.
After ten minutes stop the discussions and give them a paper

with three questions to answer:
1 Who took the lead role in the group?
2 Why did this person take such a lead?
3 Who did most of the talking and why?

Darts time

If you are in a suitable room, set up a darts board. Give each person a dart (or three) depending on the size of your group. If they score higher than five on their throw they are allowed to suggest one quality they would expect to find in a youth leader.
If it is not possible to use a darts board, ask the group to take turns in drawing a playing card from a pack. They can make their suggestion if the card number they draw is higher than five.

Produce a large list of the leadership qualities suggested: eg, friendly, happy, strong, a good listener, caring, trustworthy, loyal.

Discovery

Explain that the apostle Paul also produced a list of leadership qualities, because he wanted to see them in Timothy, one of his trainee leaders.
Hand out duplicated or photocopied sheets of 1 Timothy 3:1–7.
Ask them to get into groups of four or five (be definite now!), read the sheet and make a list of all the qualities Paul wanted to see in a leader. The groups should also give a one-sentence explanation of each quality. Give them eighteen minutes for this.
Bring the groups back together again and ask each in turn to give one quality they thought Paul was asking for. Write these up on a large sheet of paper. The list given below will help you to check out their findings. Put these alongside the list you drew up from the 'dart' throwing.

PAUL'S GUIDELINES ON LEADERSHIP			
Temperate	(1 Timothy 3:2)	Gentle	(3:3)
Self-controlled	(3:2)	Not quarrelsome	(3:3)
Respectable	(3:2)	Not a money lover	(3:3)
Hospitable	(3:2)	Good with family	(3:4)
Able to teach	(3:2)	Not a recent convert	(3:6)
Not a drunkard	(3:3)	Has a good reputation	(3:7)

Crunch time

Now hand out photocopied 'score sheets' like the one below and ask the group to do two things:

1 Give themselves marks out of ten for all the leadership qualities listed.

2 Give **you** marks out of ten for each quality.

They can add qualities to the list which they think should be there. Tell them that **you** want to be a better leader and that their honesty would be appreciated. The papers are to be anonymous. When they have finished they should hand their papers back to you.

QUALITY	MARKS OUT OF TEN	
	Me	Youth leader
Temperate		
Self-controlled		
Respectable		
Hospitable		
(add others)		

Prayer

Tell them that a person who is eager to be a leader 'desires a noble task' (1 Timothy 3:1) and that leadership is something that needs hard work and dedication.

Spend time in prayer for all those who are in leadership positions within the youth group and church, as well as for national leaders.

Final note

Discouraged? I hope not. Your young people's responses and the marks they gave you for your leadership qualities are relative in nature and only reflect their feelings now.

Final final note

Develop now (preferably yesterday) a scheme to train your potential up-and-coming-leaders.

I live in a potential war-zone in the Middle East, with troops massed only three kilometres from our home. The United Nations are in between, trying to keep the peace and to keep 'us' away from 'them'.

One morning at 5.45 we were woken by the sound of heavy artillery fire. Jumping out of bed I peered through our shutters looking to see if anyone else was panicking.

To my amazement no one seemed to have stirred and I wondered if I should be the hero to wake them. But I went back to bed instead. Then Amy, one of my daughters, rushed into our bedroom, opened a drawer and pulled out her passport. Her explanation? She needed to get to an airport to escape! Later I discovered that the guns were celebrating the president's birthday! I hope he will keep to candles in future!

During previous fighting, however, people had fled from their homes in terror, never to return to them, **never to see their possessions again**.

This session asks us to consider what makes our lives worth living.

PREPARATION

Knapsacks at the ready

Attempt to get all your group to bring some form of bag to your next meeting. Failing that, arrange to have a number of plastic bags available.

The last seven minutes

Hand out about fifteen pieces of paper to each person, along with a pen. Describe a scene similar to the one above. Each person is to imagine that he or she has only seven minutes to take a last look at their house and possessions before the invading army arrives. Each manages to grab a sportsbag or rucksack and can dash round the house in the seven minutes picking up things he or she would want to take. Ask them to imagine their own homes/rooms and, when you say 'go', to write down what things they would take (one per piece of paper given them.) They should then deposit them in their rucksacks.

Give them checks on time as you go along, having taken their watches away beforehand, to add extra tension.

When the seven-minute alarm has gone give them three extra minutes and five other pieces of paper. Ask them to add those other 'things' they would lose if they had to leave their home and country now – like lost relationships, career opportunities, goals, etc. These should be specific and added to their sacks.

Discussion

Ask the group the following questions and encourage discussion.

1 Could you live with just those things which you have collected in a hurry? Can you begin a new life with these?

2 If you had to throw ten of these things away which ones would go and why? (Get each person to put them in the bin.)

Explain

Explain that we often see ourselves in terms of how we think others see us. What do they think we are worth? How much do our friends and parents value our friendship? What do we have that somebody else can use?

For example, we hear of relationships breaking up because one partner has found someone else, leaving the other person feeling 'used'. Some people lavish gifts on their friends and relatives thinking that will make those people value the giver. At school we go along with our friends' activities even though they are sometimes wrong, simply because we don't want to lose their friendship. Some people have an ambition to be famous, because then they think they will be 'somebody'.

Self worth

Here are some better guidelines to help group members evaluate their self worth.

Ask yourself about what you do and say:

1 Is it **lasting**?
Make comparisons with God's love which is everlasting. Whatever happens to us in the future God is faithful and will never stop loving us.
   Discuss Romans 8:38–39 with your group.

2 Is it the **best expression** of myself?
Do those things which you do lead to growth in you as a person: spiritually, mentally, physically and emotionally?
   Discuss Romans 6:16 with your group. God wants the very best for us and wants people to love us and for us to love them for who they are now. He wants us to grow to maturity in developed relationships which create self worth and value.

3 Does it contribute to my deepest feelings of **self worth**? God cares for you and wants you to be 'good' for your own sake.
   Discuss Romans 5:6–11. God, by his Spirit, contributes to your self worth by giving you new values.
   Read Galatians 5:22,23. Have written out on pieces of paper the 'fruit' mentioned in Galatians 5, and drop some of this into everyone's sack.

We threw out thirty-six plastic sacks of unwanted articles, some of it rubbish. But it must be said that it was important rubbish at the time. 'It's something which I'm sure will be useful' was a phrase often heard in our house, and I hate to admit to it but I was probably the main culprit.

Moving house is one thing but we moved country. The Red Cross and other charities seemed to do well out of us as we deposited numerous sacks on their doorstep in the middle of the night. The timing was due to the hour of completing the clearance and to the urge to get rid of it (them) **now** 'before we change our minds'.

But what a relief! What a fantastic feeling once it was finished! When we got married we made a decision that we would never have any article that we would not be happy to dispose of (give away) if necessary in the case of a major house move. It was a conscious decision and one that we often reminded ourselves of, particularly when we bought yet another thing for the home.

Well, it nearly worked. All except eighteen boxes of books, an old 'Singer' sewing machine and some toys arrived in our new country of residence.

So what did we learn? What I'm hoping your teenagers will learn; that it is a fantastic feeling when we act on Jesus' words in Matthew 6:25–34 and trust him for our possessions.

PREPARATION

Prepare your group the week before by asking them to bring their most precious possessions, those which mean a lot to them. Suggest that they bring several items.

They could be sentimental things, cuddly toys, special books, hi-fi equipment, ring(s) which someone has given to them, etc. Do not be naive about temptation of theft. If any of them had the courage they could even bring their close friend(s), parents, and family members (even Granny).

PROGRAMME

If not too personal (like Granny) the articles should be displayed with a name tag showing their owner.

Either in groups or all together (the latter is preferable if your group know each other well enough), each person should select two articles which they have brought with them and explain why they are so precious to them. Keep this semi-serious.

I've hired a van to bring the rest of my most precious possessions!

30

In groups

Ask them to answer the following questions:

1 What would you feel like if any of these articles was stolen from you?
2 Have you ever had anything stolen from you which was very special to you? What was it and how did you feel?
3 Why are things and people important to us?
4 If you had to give up one of the articles you brought, which one would you give up?

Together

Bring the whole group together again and share the answers given in the smaller units.

Read Matthew 13:44–46 and ask the groups to spend eleven minutes paraphrasing it in the light of their earlier discussions about their most treasured possessions.

Ask that a few people read out their versions of this passage.

Explain

Explain that all that we have belongs to God; that there is nothing that we own, not any friendship or relationship, which does not ultimately belong to God.

As soon as we offer them to God, God does two things:

1 He begins to tell us what things are really good for us. He shows us, for instance, what things (or people) are holding us back from serving him. Remember that God is the creator of good things and likes to be **positive** with us in what we have and what we do.

2 Once we consciously give our possessions to him then he asks us to become managers and manageresses for him, to use our gifts, talents and things for his service. He also asks us to remember that he may call for an article to be given away to somebody else who has greater need than we do, or to be given up in some other way.

To understand that you own nothing and that you are simply looking after it for God gives you a **fantastically new perspective** and **a means of using your gifts more wisely**.

Why not ask your group to be very religious on Monday morning? Ask them to meet you for breakfast and prayer before school/college/work.

If this is a bit too demanding, then make it a Saturday or Sunday morning, early enough for those who have other commitments not to have an excuse for missing it.

PREPARATION

If it is summer you could cook breakfast outside. This will mean that you, as organizer, will need to get up very early – or delegate the cooking to 'those types' who are at their best very early.

PROGRAMME

On site sing a little bit, read John 21:1–14 and share your breakfast together. Depending on your church tradition and the participants, you may wish to have a very simple communion/breaking of bread service alongside your breakfast.

Pray in the open air, with eyes open, thanking God for being God. This can be something very special and should be encouraged.

The moment of truth

And there's more. . .

Now you are up, the rest of the day is yours! . . . until **midnight**, when you could hold another brief prayer 'vigil'.

A 'daylight to darkness' day can be very spiritually challenging, and would certainly be something the group never forgets!

SPECIAL
OCCASIONS

Christ in Christmas

32

Christmas is coming! It may be a few weeks away but Christmas – the celebration of Christ's birth – is something to look forward to!

Here is a gentle but positive run-up to Christmas day. The theme is the incarnation – Jesus taking the form of humanity.

PROGRAMME

Person Friday

This is an exercise in communication. Choose two or three volunteers to be explorers. Give them a card, or several cards, each with a 'how to' or 'what is' on it (see box for details of cards).

The explorers have to imagine they have just met Person Friday, who has not been influenced by anyone from any other island and has no knowledge of anything except sun, sea, sand and jungle.

They then have to explain to Person Friday how to make a pot of tea, use a biro, etc. The rest of the group play Person Friday and must think themselves into the part, asking questions like 'what is ink?' 'Why do you want to drink hot water and leaves?' etc.

Alternatively, choose one volunteer to be Person Friday and have the rest of the group doing the explanations.

CARDS

HOW TO...
1   make a pot of tea
2   use a biro
3   play football
4   fly in an aeroplane
5   use a typewriter

WHAT IS...?
1   an explosion
2   a bar of soap
3   a motor car
4   electricity
5   a lamp post

After about twenty minutes of hilarity, hand out a few cards with more subjects, but this time even more abstract: God, love, hate, mercy, death, life, Holy Spirit.

Explain

Explain in your own words that:
● Communicating everyday objects and happenings is not always easy. For example, even professional journalists seem to write different versions of the same real-life events.
● It is very difficult to understand things that we have not seen, heard, tasted, smelt or felt; things which may be described to us but which we have not experienced with our senses.
● It is very difficult to describe God to people. It is almost impossible to express what we mean by his love. It is bordering on the eccentric to talk about the Holy Spirit in a world in which 'scientific objectivity' is so important.
● How can we express what God is like, then, unless we show him working in and through history, becoming flesh and living among us?

32

If I were God. . .
Give each member a pen and some paper, and eight minutes to write down some notes to complete a paragraph which begins: 'If I were God I would have communicated to the world by. . .'

Discuss the suggestions they come up with. Give reasons why some of the suggestions would work while others might not. Allow for plenty of interaction.

Why Jesus?
List some of their more constructive thinking on a board or OHP. Was Jesus' life and death just a publicity stunt? But then again, he came quietly into a poor home, etc. Explain that to discover God we need to discover Jesus. For others to discover Jesus we need to be like him.

WHO WAS JESUS?
Hand out some cards with Bible verses on, to be looked up and read aloud (see below).

WHO WAS JESUS?	
John 10:30	uniquely one with God
John 14:9:	the image of the Father
John 4:26:	the promised Messiah
John 14:6:	the only way to God
John 8:46:	sinless
Matthew 11:29	humble

Planning ahead
Plan activities which will reflect Jesus as the Son of God this Christmas. Bear in mind that most people are as ignorant about God as our Man/Girl Friday was about tea-making.

Our 'island' man/woman is actually better off than most of our non-Christian friends, because news of Jesus is all so new. In our country our friends and family begin with their own assumptions about Jesus which may be nothing more than folklore.

Plan to communicate the real Jesus this Christmas – you have time!

If I were God, I would have communicated to the world by...
1. Zapping them with an earthquake/comet/black hole
2. Shouting at them from a cloud in a deep American accent (like in the films)
3. Getting other humans to deliver my message to the world
4. Flying saucers
5. Becoming the helpless baby of a poor, unknown peasant couple

JR leaves the briefcase in the office as he dashes to see if Jack is OK.

As he enters one elevator, Sue Ellen arrives in the other, walks into JR's office and boom! Meanwhile, Jack's sister is blown up by JR's arch enemy – are Jack's sister and Sue Ellen dead?

But good news – Pam marries Mark (at last) without being gunned down. But she wakes up on the first morning of her honeymoon to find ... yes, you've guessed it ... not Mark but Bobby.

I like and dislike Dallas at the same time. Perhaps what I really like is the creativity of the script writers – all that high drama.

High drama is what the Christmas story is all about. The dramatic unfolding of the birth of Jesus is not only good creative prose but a true life story of the most important event in history.

There is Mary, an adolescent of between twelve and fifteen years; Joseph, the older, hard-working, semi-skilled carpenter; Zechariah, the doubting priest, the father of the hairy, locust-eating John the baptizer; Herod, the tyrant who killed most of his family because of his fear that they would oust him.

The events and the larger-than-life characters in the story of Jesus' birth out-Dallas Dallas. But that's where the similarity ends.

For your youth group session on Christ's birth and his message of peace and unity to all people, start with some high drama.

PROGRAMME

High drama

Either make up a soap opera script with characters your group know and build in the Christmas story (see box for Bible references), or make a soap script out of the story itself. You could do this by having a few members of your group read out their character's lines, perhaps with a musical accompaniment, or write out the whole soap script and then divide it up onto cards and give each member of the group a card to read out in turn.

Coke cans

Read John 10:10. Then take a can of coke or any fizzy drink in a bottle, shake it and take the top off. (Watch out for the wallpaper.) Explain that Christ through his birth, death and resurrection, brought us a life which just bubbles and bursts with the energy of God and gives a unity among Christians that is thicker and stronger than blood ties.

Sugar lumps

Prepare a large jug of hot water and give each person a sugar lump. (They are not to eat it.) Explain that unity is building lots of different lumps together. Jesus mixes our lumps into one body. Ask people to put their lumps into the jug. Mix it up until they are all dissolved. Read John 17:22–23 to them.

Coffee filter

Get two jugs and some coffee filters. Fill one jug with muddy water and then filter it into the other jug. Change the filter and keep repeating the process until the water is clear. Explain that our unity is like a filter against the devil. Together we gradually weaken and dilute the influence of the devil in society. However, we need each others' support and encouragement.

Castrol GTX

Obtain a rusty nut and bolt (leave them out in the rain). Try to fit the bolt into the nut. Hopefully it will be difficult. Squirt some oil onto them, rub it in with a cloth and then gently screw the nut and bolt together.

Unity among Christians is a natural product of the Spirit of Jesus in our lives. It is like the oil reducing the friction in our relationships and so producing essential and natural spiritual unity. Read the group Psalm 133:1–2.

33

Furniture

Ask someone in your group to move a piece of furniture to a new position. The object should be of such a size or weight that it actually needs three or more people. When the person fails to move it alone seek the assistance of others and supervise the 'removal'. Ask your group which person moved the piece of furniture. Their response will show that no one individual moved it but the joint energy and initiative of all participants made it possible. Explain the importance of unity of effort under the supervision of Christ.

Read out John 17:22 again, and follow it with the saying which Ronald Reagan, when President, was reputed to keep on his desk: 'There is no limit to what a man can do or where he can go if he doesn't mind who gets the credit'.

Communion

Depending on your denomination, you may wish to show your unity by participating in communion together. If you do, keep it simple.

Read the following to the group: 'At Christmas time families and friends meet in a very special way. Barriers are broken down; people are "nice" to each other. Christians are *not* called to be "nice" to each other. Through Christ they are called to be "one". We may differ in our views, in the way we pray or worship, we may find it difficult to relate with people from other races or cultures, but the heartbeat of our faith and witness is our unity.'

This Christmas, put into practice the message of Jesus' coming. Make up for any quarrels you have had, and affirm your unity as a group.

Intermingle appropriate traditional carols with relevant choruses, as you finish the meeting. Celebrate with cans or bottles of Coke (shaken first)!

THE CHRISTMAS STORY

Luke 1:5–23:	Zechariah, priest on duty in Temple, receives a vision and is struck dumb.
Luke 1:57–66:	Old woman Elizabeth gives birth to child.
Luke 1:26–38:	Cousin Mary gets a visit from top angel.
Matt 1:18–24:	Mary gets reprieve from stoning.
Luke 2:1–5:	Emperor calls for tax census. Joseph takes pregnant wife to Bethlehem – eighty miles away.
Luke 2:6–7:	Son of God born in a stable.
Matt 2:16–18:	Herod kills all baby boys under two. Estimated deaths between twenty and thirty. Jesus escapes at the eleventh hour as Joseph gets message in a dream.
Matt 2:13–15:	Joseph, Mary and Jesus join refugees in Egypt.

Easter trial

34

The high court judge lifts his hammer as he prepares to give the verdict of the jury. The judgement must be 'guilty' – too much is at stake. Outside, the mob are at the door. This one man must die for the sake of the future ... for the people ... for Rome.

A similar trial is the setting for this week's session. At Easter, the most important festival in Christian history, what more powerful, dramatic way to recall those events than to re-enact the trial of Jesus with your group?

The difference is, this will not be a play rehearsed in advance – courts do not have rehearsals but they do prepare themselves in advance by reading the evidence and getting witnesses. Depending on your group's abilities you will have to give more or less briefing on how to proceed.

Try to find somewhere that will make the trial seem official and serious, like a hall or church. Arrange seating in a way that gives the impression of a courtroom.

The actors

Choose members of your youth group first and then other members of your church depending on the number of actors available. The audience could be parents, friends and church members.

Key characters

The judge, the prosecution and the defence have no actual lines to learn but they do have to do some homework. They have to read the evidence (biblical passages), prepare their cases for questioning and cross-questioning, decide which witnesses to call, etc.

The people playing these characters should be alert, able to speak well and even be entertaining.

The defence and prosecution should be encouraged to call witnesses who are not mentioned in detail in the biblical text, eg Jairus, one of the temple money changers, a temple guard, someone who saw Jesus flick a coin and talk about duty to God and Caesar, etc.

PREPARATION

Find out something of how a court proceeds, eg how the defendant is questioned by both the prosecution and the defence, how witnesses are called, etc.

CHARACTERS

Judge .... with black gown and wig

Prosecution .... suitably attired in gowns and wigs

Defence

Jury .... sitting at side

Judas .... (with money belt) key witness for the prosecution

Jesus .... the defendant, calm and watchful

Disciples .... in variety of modern dress suggesting their occupations

Pharisees

Sanhedrin .... all in modern dress suggesting they are top religious and government figures.

Pilate

Herod

Biblical evidence

The Bible verses in the box below form the key evidence for the trial and must be read and re-read by the characters in the trial.

THE TRIAL

Jesus of Nazareth is charged with blasphemy, for claiming he is the Son of God, for claiming he is the King of the Jews and for subversive anti-Rome activities.

Timing

The trial may take as long as two hours, so the judge might well call a recess for refreshments half way through

The verdict

The judge must publicly instruct the jury to find Jesus guilty before they retire to discuss their verdict. Do not warn anyone of this in advance. Allow people to respond to this statement emotionally.

AFTERWARDS

It is important that you hold a session later to discuss why certain characters answered questions in the way they did. Allow all those involved and watching to say how they felt about this and to question one another about their different responses.

This is a complicated exercise but if you rise to the challenge you will discover the planning will pay dividends.

Why not approach the local courthouse for permission to visit the courtroom one evening? Why not ask them if you can stage a mock trial of Jesus there? I'm serious! Let me know how it goes.

34

BIBLICAL EVIDENCE
Money changers	Matthew 21:12–14
Judas	Luke 22:1–6; Mark 14:43–45
Pharisees	Mark 11:27–33; 12:38–40; 14:1–2, 53–65
Temple guards	Luke 22:47–53
Peter	Mark 8:1–13, 27–30; 14:27–31, 32–50, 66–72
Sadduccees	Mark 12:18–27
James and John	Matthew 20:20–23
People	Matthew 21:8–11
Pilate	Mark 15:1–15
Soldiers	Mark 15:16–30
Simon of Cyrene	Mark 15:20–22
Herod	Luke 23:6–12
Pilate's wife	Matthew 27:19
Jesus	Matthew 27:11–14

35 Sherlock

Sometimes our young people need another angle to get them into the Bible. So why not get them to try their hand at some private detective work on the resurrection of Jesus?

PROGRAMME

The investigation

Split your group up into smaller units, giving each group the name of a national newspaper. Then give each group a notebook and one of these passages of the Bible to investigate:

The earthquake	Matthew 28:1–4
The women at the tomb	Matthew 28:1–8
Mary finds the tomb empty	John 20:1–2
Mary Magdalene tells Peter	Mark 16:9–11
Jesus appears to Mary Magdalene	John 20:10–18
Jesus appears to other women	Matthew 28:8–10
The report of the guards	Matthew 28:11–15
Jesus appears to Peter	Luke 24:33–34
Jesus appears on the Emmaus road	Luke 24:13–35

Give each group ten minutes to explore their own findings from the verses given. Then, note-book in hand, they have twenty minutes to visit their other newspaper friends to build up a complete picture of what happened.

Reporting

After this, give the 'newspapers' only twelve minutes to write up their story ready for print. Each should read out their story and the other groups should back them or challenge them when they feel it necessary.

This is a good way for your youth group to come to understand how the individual incidents of the resurrection story piece together.

Saint's party 36

It is time we turned the tables on Halloween festivities. 'Halloween' is the night before All Saints' Day, the Christian festival of 'All Hallows' on which we remember the saints of old. So let's take the emphasis off the pagan festival (Halloween) and put it back on the stories of the saints (All Saints' Day). There are saints from centuries ago, and present-day saints. You can mix dramatic readings from the early Christian 'fathers' with stories of those who have lived and died in the service of God over the last twenty years.

We're going to have a saints' party in heaven, so why not start now?!

PREPARATION

Prepare the following:

● **Invitations** in the shape of a fish (the early Christian sign). Don't forget to send them.

● **Food** labelled with saints' names, eg *St Peter's Fish Paste*; *Simon's Sausages*; *Cornelius' Pig Blanket* (sausage rolls).

● **Party games**, eg 'Spot-a-saint': As the young people come in, pin the name of a 'saint' to their backs. They are to go round asking questions to find out who they are. Keep it simple for those who are new to the scriptures. You could even wear 'masks', each with the name of a saint on it. Everybody has to treat the person behind the mask with the respect and deference due to the name shown on it. In fact it would be good to pin a summary of the saint's life to the person so that as people socialize they can communicate with them more intelligently. Each needs to talk as if he or she were the saint named on their mask. Saints are not necessarily 'dead', so include people like Mother Teresa.

PROGRAMME

What I would like to know is . . .

With the party atmosphere created in this way, bring everyone together and ask what questions they would like to pose one of the saints. Explain that saints are not limited just to the disciples or to the saints on church name boards but that all Christians are called 'saints' in the Bible (Ephesians 1:15, 18; 6:18; Romans 8:27).

Give them pieces of paper and get them to write down these questions alongside the name of a chosen saint.

Once done, arrange for these to be collected and read out the questions slowly and carefully, getting the group to answer them as they think the saints would.

36

Stories

Borrow a couple of books from your minister on early Christian martyrs (saints) and select a few stories to read out. You may need to summarize them. It would be even better to get some of your group to give dramatic readings in light of the information you give them about the respective saint. This will need to be prepared thoroughly.

Choose a couple of 'saints' from the New Testament and a couple of people that the group are aware of in the church. Give the saintly histories of all four, showing that there **are** living saints.

Challenge to sainthood

Finally, tell them that the words 'martyr' and 'witness' are the same in the Bible. Many of the early Christians found there was no difference between them. Challenge the group to sainthood in light of this. If they are wearing masks ask them to remove them now as a declaration of their own sainthood and as a sign of their own commitment to Christ.

CYPRUS MOVE

Bob and Jilly Moffett and their family have moved to Cyprus where they are working with Youth for Christ.

If Bob has helped you with the outlines and ideas in this book, then why not help them by praying for and supporting them? You could get your young people involved in this too.

For details of how you could help, please write to Bob and Jilly Moffett, c/o 64 Shrublands Avenue, Berkhamsted, Herts.

DON'T MISS . . .

Power Pack
(Scripture Union)
Thirty-six outlines on:
- The church and fellowship
- Myself and how I live
- A Christian in society
- Sharing and communicating
- Special occasions

Power Pack 2
(Scripture Union)
Thirty-three outlines:
- God, me and others
- It happens to Christians too! (Problems and difficulties)
- What about . . .? (Mind-bending issues)
- Who, me?! (Challenges to commitment)
- Special occasions

Other books by Bob and Jilly Moffett:

Crowdbreakers
(Marshall Pickering)
A book on youth leadership, with over one hundred creative games.

Crowdmakers
(Marshall Pickering)
More practical ideas for youth leaders.

A Guide to Evangelism
(Marshall Pickering)
Jointly edited with Derek Copley, Jim Smith and Clive Calver.
Practical guidelines on most forms of evangelism, with contributions from over fifty well-known evangelists and pastors.